Self-Sufficient Pottery

SELF-SUFFICIENT POTTERY

JUDY CUNNINGHAM-SMITH
& MOLLIE HERBERT

David & Charles
Newton Abbot London North Pomfret (Vt)

British Library Cataloguing in Publication Data
Cunningham-Smith, Judy
Self-sufficient pottery.
1. Pottery craft
I. Title II. Herbert, Mollie
738.1 TT920

ISBN 0-7153-7674-8

Set by Trade Linotype Limited, Birmingham
and printed in Great Britain
by Redwood Burn Ltd, Trowbridge and Esher,
for David & Charles (Publishers) Limited
Brunel House Newton Abbot Devon

Published in the United States of America
by David & Charles Inc
North Pomfret Vermont 05053 USA

Contents

Metric Conversion Tables

LENGTH: 1cm = 0.394in

cm	0.5	1	2	3	4	5	10	20	25	50	100
in	0.2	0.39	0.79	1.18	1.58	1.97	3.94	7.87	9.84	19.7	39.4

WEIGHT: 1kg = 2.2lb

kg	1	2	3	4	5	10	20	25	50	100
lb	2.2	4.4	6.6	8.8	11	22	44	55	110	220

TEMPERATURE: to convert Centigrade to Fahrenheit, multiply by 9, divide the result by 5 and add 32

°C	100	200	300	400	500	600	700
°F	212	392	572	752	932	1112	1292

°C	800	900	1000	1100	1200	1300
°F	1472	1652	1832	2012	2192	2372

Acknowledgements

Our sincere thanks go to all who have made this book possible, and especially to Doig and Ruth Simmonds, who gave us so much help and encouragement in our adventures with making and firing pots in the African tradition and persuaded us to write the book; to Emeritus Professor P. Stoy, who edited our script as we wrote; to Annette Fowler, who taught us to be potters and teachers; to Devon County Education Committee and Colin Jolliffe of the Exmouth Adult Education Centre, who give us much encouragement in our methods of teaching; and to the lending library staff of Exeter Central Library, who keep us supplied with books about pottery for loan to students and introduced us to our publishers through David St John Thomas's book *Non-Fiction: A Guide to Writing and Publishing*.

We are grateful to John Picton of the Ethnography Department of the British Museum and to Michael Cardew for advice on African methods of making and firing pots; to Ronald J. Slawson of Acme Marls Ltd for information on clays; to all suppliers mentioned in the book, who have helped in various ways, and to those who have supplied illustrations; to the South West Gas Company Industrial Section for advice on the makeshift gas kiln; to Pinhoe Brickworks of Westbrick Products Ltd for supplying us with brick marl; and to Russell Cowan Pty Ltd for permission to use the drawings of the makeshift gas kiln by Barnacoat and Polglase.

Finally, special thanks to Denise Bates, Joan Grigg and Cherrill Bailey for babysitting, and to our husbands for their patience while routines were upset and dining-rooms taken over as offices; to John Herbert for his help and advice in the construction of the updraft and makeshift kilns; and, last but not least, to all our students, past and present, for the fun we have in working together and for providing the 'raw material' for this book.

The line drawings are by Judy Cunningham-Smith, and photographs were supplied by the following:

B. Allan: 1, 5-7, 11, 13-16, 19, 26-7, 33-4, 43-6, 48, 50, 55, 57-8, 62, 64, 100, 104, 106-7, 108, 111-16
Michael Coleridge: 59
Freddie Collins: 54, 56
Judy Cunningham-Smith: 38
Mollie Herbert: 12, 22, 28, 36-7, 39-42, 47, 51-2, 66, 88
Wm. A. Meyer Ltd: 95
Doig Simmonds: 60, 87, 105
Ruth Simmonds: 86
Ian Wolfe: 101

Foreword

I have known Mollie Herbert since 1952 when she and her husband first came to my pottery classes at the School of Art and Science in Frome, Somerset, where I was then teaching. Both Mollie and her husband showed unusual promise and interest both in the making of pots and in the whole process of conditioning clay, glazing and firing. It was on some of the afternoon visits to the Frome pottery that Mollie brought her daughter Judy, then aged three.

Later I was able to recommend Mollie Herbert as a teacher of pottery to the soldier cadets stationed at Corsham in Wiltshire. This was the beginning of her pottery teaching career. In the following years she gained experience in teaching various groups of people, many of them handicapped.

In the autumn of 1972 the Camperdown Pottery Studio was started as a teaching centre, and Mollie began classes there as part of the adult education programme for Exmouth. Judy Cunningham-Smith now joined her mother in the teaching and, when the number of classes was increased to cope with demand, she was also accepted by the Devon Education Committee as an official teacher at the Camperdown Pottery.

It was while teaching at the Camperdown Pottery that Mollie and Judy developed two unique (as far as I know) schemes of work. The first is a three-year course, during which time the students are taught all the techniques and given all the practical experience in the making of hand-built pottery, right through from the care of the clay to the building, decorating, firing and glazing of the pots, thus making them self-sufficient potters.

The second scheme sprang from an idea started when Judy was in Antigua in the Caribbean on her honeymoon, and met an old blind woman who made her living building pots by hand for firing in an open bonfire. On returning to England to find power restrictions in force, Judy suggested that, rather than close the pottery, they should try firing some of the Camperdown pots in the same way. This activity proved so rewarding that they made a study of the technique of 'bush firing', as they have come to call it, and have developed part of the course around it. Not only do the students make beautiful pots using methods adapted from those used in Nigeria, but the pots are now fired with almost 100 per cent success in the bush fire and with very satisfying results as to colour and texture. Students are also using African techniques to decorate and burnish their pots. The result is work of a strikingly mature and original kind.

Annette Fowler, NNFF

Introduction

In our own studio we run a three-year course sponsored by Devon County Council Adult Education Committee. As tutors, our aim has been to teach people to be potters for their own pleasure and not necessarily for commercial gain. The students come from all walks of life and ages run from sixteen to well over eighty. At the end of the course most of them are capable of running a pottery and some of them have in fact set up their own studios. They may join the ceramic club in Exmouth, which has been formed by our past students, and use the pottery which they have built. Others prefer to concentrate on using the methods of construction and firing adapted from those used in Africa.

It is our aim in this book to lay out that information which we have found necessary to start a person on the path to becoming, if necessary, entirely self-sufficient in the way that the native potters of Africa are independent of modern mechanisation.

It is important that pottery should be a pleasure rather than a chore. Criticism should be ignored unless it concerns the construction of a piece and

1. Jane Jackson, 'pewter effect' glazed pinched earthenware bottle, 22.5cm

is given by a tutor or other qualified person. If an article fails to please its creator it should be destroyed. Confidence in one's work is increased if the courage can be found to destroy anything which is unsatisfactory. If one is unsure how a piece should develop, it is a good idea to cover it with polythene or a damp cloth and return to it later. The impression received on seeing it again should be accepted. It is unwise to ask for the opinions of others, as everybody has a different set of tastes and ideas.

For the harmonious running of a pottery, whether that of a single potter or a group, the following principles should be understood: the preparation of clay, how to use it and how to reconstitute it; how to make glazes and how to apply them; how to load, fire and unload kilns; how to keep a pottery clean and to be economical with materials.

If coiling, pinching and slab work with clay are mastered, those who are mechanically minded will find that throwing comes naturally; if not, it is best forsaken for hand-building methods in which there is no limit to what can be achieved.

Nothing is impossible with clay until it has been attempted and proved so. Any ideas should be tried out because many discoveries come from these ideas, even though the result may bear little or no resemblance to the original concept.

1 Preparation, Care and Economy of Clay

If one's aim is to dig and prepare local clays, it is necessary to understand a certain amount about their nature and origins in order that a great deal of time and effort is not wasted over unsuitable ones. The following will give the potter who seeks to find his own materials some idea of where to look and for what.

The term 'clay' is used by different people to mean different things. The potter uses the word to refer to any material that will form a plastic mass with water and which, after drying, can be fired to form a hard brittle material that is no longer affected by water.

Geologically speaking, there are very few pure clays. These are seldom used for the production of ceramics as they tend to be sticky and to shrink excessively during drying and firing. Consequently, if they are to be used at all, they are mixed with other materials to modify their plastic, drying and firing properties. Such mixtures are usually known as 'bodies'.

China clay is one of the few pure clays which can be used for ceramics. It consists of almost pure kaolinite which is a 'clay mineral'. Owing to the relatively large size of the kaolinite crystals, china clays tend not to be very plastic and are thus best suited to making slip-casting bodies. These are used in liquid form for pouring into plaster moulds, and are extensively employed in the manufacture of mass-produced commercial ceramics.

China clays are found where they were formed during the process of cooling of the rock by the breakdown of feldspars, particularly in granite. Since the quartz and mica, which together with the feldspar make up the granite, are still present in an unchanged form, a very complicated system of washing has to be used to extract varying amounts of these substances, according to the purpose for which the clay is to be used. Deposits are mined commercially and, because of this and the washing processes necessary, it is not practical for the self-sufficient potter to dig his own china clay.

Kaolinite is also formed by weathering on the surface where granite is exposed. However, this is washed away as fast as it is formed and, along with other minerals picked up by the water, is deposited in shallow seas or large lakes where it forms mud deposits. These deposits eventually form the ball clays which can contain between 20 and 80 per cent of kaolinite.

Ball clay. Where rivers flow into large lakes or shallow seas, the minerals they carry are deposited—the larger particles near the shore and the finest material further out—to form a mud. This sediment of mud can build up to an immense thickness. Of course, it is not possible to use the mud from the sea bed, but where earth movements have raised the deposits above sea level and compressed them to form clays, then they are of great value to the potter.

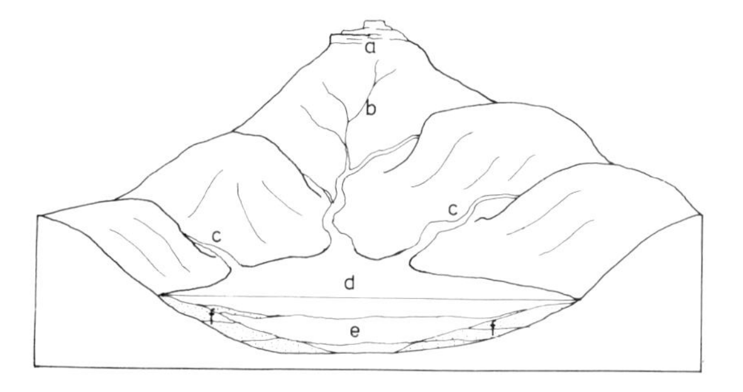

2. The formation of ball clays: *a* granite tor; *b* streams carrying kaolinite away; *c* streams carrying other minerals from different sources; *d* basin of deposition; *e* muds which will become ball clays; *f* sands and gravels

As illustration 3 shows, where there is sand or gravel there is a good chance that clay will be found somewhere nearby. It is a good idea to enquire at quarries where sand is dug whether there is any clay in the vicinity. Clay is of no value to the sand and gravel merchant, and the manager may well be only too pleased to direct the potter to any deposits nearby.

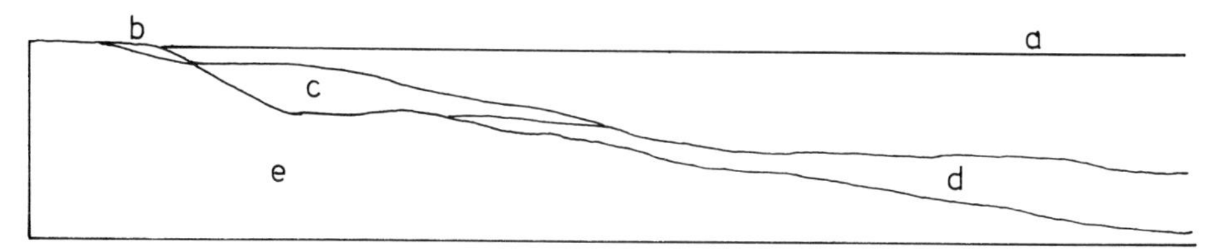

3. The deposition of muds and sand in shallow seas and lakes: *a* water level; *b* gravel; *c* sand; *d* mud; *e* bedrock

Sometimes it is possible to collect clay from the shoreline of a lake after a drought, but this does tend to be highly contaminated with organic material. If the clay proves to be workable but contains too many organic impurities to be fired safely, then it should be dug and left in a heap somewhere out of the way to 'weather' so that the organic elements can decompose and be leached out. The same should be done when clay is dug from near the surface, where roots and soil can be present.

Where the soil is sticky and 'heavy' to work, there is often a good usable clay about one metre below.

Mud from the bends of rivers, or the spits formed where two rivers merge, can be collected when water levels are low. This mud has to be subjected to the weathering process before it can be used for making pottery, but it is a good regular source of material if it proves to be workable when tested.

Coal-measure clays. Beneath each layer (seam) of coal there is one of clay. These clays vary considerably in composition and are therefore of little interest to the commercial potter. However, the variations in texture and fired colour, from light buff to almost black, are welcomed by the studio potter whose work is aimed at individuality rather than mass-produced uniformity.

Those clays which underlie the coal were once layers of mud in which the coal-forming vegetation grew. They can usually be fired to very high temperatures because the vegetation used up the alkalis and most of the lime present. It is these clays which, when found in quantities worth mining, are used to produce firebricks, as the lack of alkalis enables them to withstand very high temperatures without fusion or distortion. Generally, the deposits are too small to be worked commercially and are therefore dumped as waste if they are removed from the coal mine at all. A well-placed word might provide the enterprising self-sufficient potter with a supply of clay from a local coal tip for the rest of his potting life.

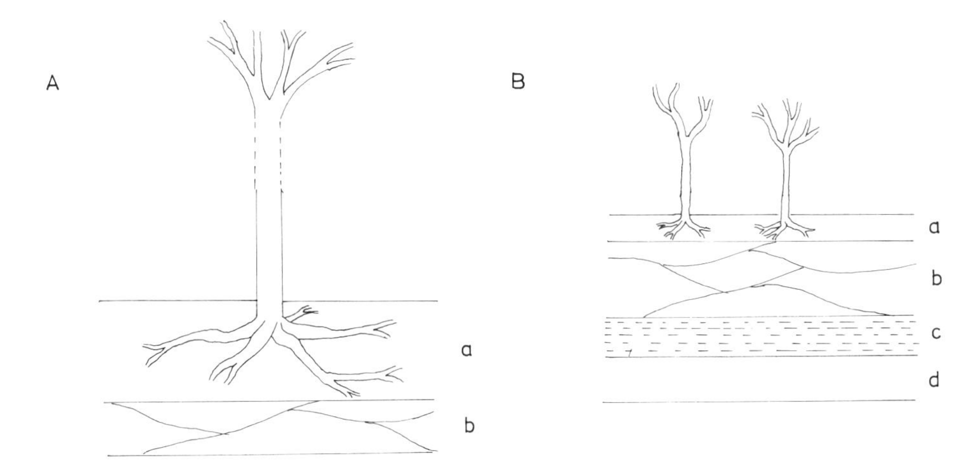

4. The formation of coal-measure clays: *Aa* swamp with vegetation growing in mud; *Ab* sandstone. *Ba* new mud left by receding floods, vegetation beginning to grow again; *Bb* sand deposited during flooding; *Bc* coal forming from vegetation *Aa*; *Bd* mud compressed to form clay

Once the coal-making swamps became permanently flooded, there followed a period where alternate layers of mud and sandstone were laid down. These did not have the alkalis removed and are therefore often much lower-firing, producing the 'pottery clays' such as are found in the area around the Staffordshire Potteries. The deposits tend to be thicker and are therefore more often mined commercially.

There are often ironstone nodules present in the coal-measure clays, produced by bacterial action during the decay of the roots of the coal-forming vegetation. These nodules cause black craters to form in the clay when it is fired. The studio potter can remove all but the finest of these by making the clay into a slurry of the consistency of thin cream and passing it through a fine sieve, as described on p. 15. Those nodules remaining will be so small that they will not cause cratering but will produce a fine speckled effect in the fired clay. This speckling cannot be relied on, however, as the occurrence of the nodules is completely random. If a consistent speckled body is required it is better to produce it by mixing a measured quantity of 'spangles' (magnetite) into a good quality ball clay.

Most of these clays can be used without modification, but if necessary their working properties can be altered by the addition of inert material, usually in the form of powdered prefired clay, known as 'grog' or 'filler'. The firing temperature can be lowered a little by the addition of feldspar or by mixing with a lower-firing clay.

Red clays are very fine-textured earthenware clays which contain a high proportion of iron. They are laid down in deep ocean water and the deposits are often very thick. They are used for the production of terracotta, Rockingham and similar ware, and are invaluable to the studio potter for modelling and hand-building because of their fine texture and good working properties.

The ball clays, coal-measure clays and red earthenware clays are the most important to the self-sufficient potter, but there are several others which should be recognised, if only in order that they may be avoided.

Boulder clay is produced by the grinding action of glaciers against the rocks over which they pass. It takes its name from the great number of large rounded lumps of rock present within it. This type of clay is found in large quantities wherever there has been glacial action. Its composition depends entirely on the rocks over which the glacier travelled, but generally this type of clay is suitable only for brick-making.

Marl, strictly speaking, is the term applied to clays containing a high proportion of calcium carbonate. These are generally found associated with limestone, and are unsuitable for making ceramics, although they may occasionally be used for brick-making.

To the potter the term marl applies to any coarse plastic clay, generally in the form of a body containing a large quantity of coarse grog.

Once a deposit of clay has been located, it should be tested for plasticity. See if it can be pinched out to form a small bowl about 5cm across. If it will hold this shape and does not crumble when worked, it shows promise of being a good usable clay. Test-fire several of these small bowls over a range of temperatures. Some clays distort between 800°C and 900°C; these are ideal for bush firing, but if they are to be fired to a higher temperature in a kiln, then a filler such as silica sand or grog must be added to them.

When 'pop out' or 'splintering' occurs during firing, it is usually due to the presence of lumps of impurity, which must be removed by filtering if the clay is to be of any use to the potter.

5. *Top*: Marny Millard, figures in red earthenware. *Left*: 23cm. *Right*: tallest, 30cm. *Bottom left*: Marny Millard, figures in white earthenware. *Bottom right*: Carol Jones, figure in red earthenware with glazes painted over a base glaze, 16cm

There is only one way to clean clay and that is to turn it into a slurry and pass it through a sieve. To do this the clay must first be dried out by leaving it in the sun or in a warm room or airing cupboard. When it is dry it should be hammered into a coarse powder and added to twice its volume of water in a suitable bowl or bucket, stirred well and left to soak for a few days. The next step is to stir it well and then brush it through a 60 mesh sieve—a nylon washing-up brush and a metal kitchen sieve are excellent for this purpose—and return it to a bowl or bucket to settle out.

When the clay has settled the clear water can be ladled or siphoned off and the clay spread out 3cm thick on a sheet of polythene or a stone slab and covered with sheets of paper from a glossy magazine which will absorb water but not stick to the clay. The paper will help to dry the clay and will prevent a hard crust forming on the surface; change the paper as it becomes wet.

When the clay is still sticky to the touch, up to 50 per cent by volume of filler such as grog can be added to widen its firing range and increase its strength. This also helps to dry out the clay.

The addition of certain fillers to low-firing clays will produce excellent bodies for bush firing. These are mentioned in Chapter 5.

When it is dry enough to handle easily, the clay should be kneaded well and formed into blocks about 20cm × 10cm × 10cm. Each block should be wedged to consolidate the clay and expel any air. This is done by throwing it repeatedly on to the bench with a sharp slap, the four long sides followed by the two ends. Continue wedging each block until there are no air pockets left. This can be checked by cutting the block in half; when the block shows perfect the two halves can be thrown back together and the block shaped up for storage.

Another method of wedging clay is to wrap the block in strong polythene and beat it evenly on all sides with a block of wood or a rolling-pin. This method is not so strenuous but is equally effective, making it ideal for the physically handicapped.

Digging and preparing one's own clay can be very rewarding. However, an excellent range of prepared bodies can be obtained from a number of suppliers. Details of these, including their firing properties, can be found in the suppliers' catalogues.

Most pottery is fired twice. The first firing leaves the clay porous but unaffected by water. This is known as a bisque or biscuit firing; the term 'biscuit' is also used for the fired ware. The temperature at which this state is reached varies between 800°C and 1150°C. The porous nature of the body at this stage makes it possible to apply to it a coating of powdered minerals which, when fired to a temperature at which they vitrify, form a coating of glaze on the surface of the body. This second firing is referred to as the glost firing.

The glost firing for an earthenware clay must be below 1150°C, as above this temperature the clay will vitrify and distort. Stoneware clays can be fired up to 1250°C without distortion. Above 1150°C they become impermeable even if they are not glazed.

Prepared bodies are usually supplied in 20 or 25kg plastic bags. For hand-built work, this clay should not need to be wedged before use as it will have been mechanically de-aired ('pugged').

Be kind to your clay. Do not let it dry out, and always rewrap the main block after cutting a piece off. It should be cut with a cheese wire—a length of wire or nylon gut with a handle at each end—or, if it is a coarsely grogged body, with a large knife. Do not pull lumps off, as this produces a ragged surface on the main block as well as on the piece taken—which, unless it is wedged before use, will contain air pockets and be uneven in texture.

By gentle persuasion clay can be made to take almost any shape, but it should not be forced. Forcing may cause all sorts of troubles, as it creates variations in texture which lead to weaknesses in the work, and these can make themselves manifest at any time during drying and firing. In slab work, for example, if the clay is uneven in texture this may give rise to severe warping and uneven shrinkage.

If clay is overworked it gets 'tired', losing its plasticity and starting to crumble. To avoid having to work it too much, cut it with a cheese wire into lumps as near as possible to the required final shape: that is to say, a thin slice if rolling out, a cube if pinching, a long narrow lump for coiling. This applies particularly to fine-textured bodies.

Economy is very important in these days of high prices. Any scraps of clay produced while working should immediately be squashed together and kept damp in a polythene bag or wrapped in a damp rag. This clay should be wedged and, if not used in the completion of the work in hand, should be carefully welded back on to the main block. Bear in mind, too, that every unsuccessful piece coming out of the kiln is a waste of materials. It is important, therefore, that there should be no air pockets in a finished article, as air trapped within clay expands on heating; since the clay will not stretch like a balloon it will shatter, often spoiling other pots in its vicinity, and if the kiln is electric the elements may be damaged. All joins must be perfectly made, taking care that no air is trapped between the joined surfaces. A bad join will open up when the pot shrinks during drying and firing.

6. John Herbert, coiled earthenware bottles. *Left*: double-dipped, brown over green, 22cm. *Right*: matt glaze, 27cm

There are other ways in which one can economise. Clay which is too hard to use but not actually dry should be cut up into ½cm slices which are then dipped in water and made into a neat pile, wrapped in polythene and thumped evenly on all sides with a rolling pin or a block of wood. If it is then stored in a cool place for a few days before being unwrapped, it will be ready for kneading and wedging.

Unfired dry clay, such as discarded pots, should be hammered into a coarse powder and reconstituted in the way described for cleaning and preparing newly dug clay.

Cleanliness in the pottery is essential; the prospect of having to wash up before one can start work is guaranteed to make one's inspiration die. It is even worse if the mess was left by someone else. Clean *everything* after use so that different clays and glazes do not become mixed and contaminated.

2 Coiling, Pinching and Building with Slabs

Coiling

We introduce this method first because we think it is the quickest and easiest way to learn to handle and control clay.

When making coils it is essential that one has enough room on the bench for working, so that nothing gets in the way of the coil as it lengthens. The working surface should be clean and smooth—a vinyl-top table, for instance, or a sheet of hardboard or chipboard.

To make a coil, cut from the main block a long strip of clay, square in section, and squeeze it into a cylindrical shape. Next, place it on the work surface, rest the palms of the hands lightly on the centre and roll the clay backwards and forwards using the whole length of the hands. At the same time, move the hands out along the length of the clay, spreading the fingers with the forward movement and bringing them together on the reverse. Repeat this action until the coil is the size required.

The coil must complete at least a full revolution in each direction, otherwise it will become oval, making the rolling very difficult. Should this happen, pat the coil back into a round shape before restarting the rolling.

The pressure of the hands should be very light and more of a guide than a push, their movement outwards causing the thinning and lengthening of the coil. If the pressure of one hand is greater than that of the other the coil will become thinner at that end. To remedy this, either turn the coil end for end when it becomes apparent, or use only one hand to do the rolling.

Care must be taken to ensure that the ends of the coil do not become hollow by checking them regularly during the rolling and, at the first sign of the clay's forming into a tube, nipping off the hollow parts.

Hot dry hands can cause the clay to dry out and crack. If this happens, moisten the hands with a little water, smooth out the cracks and take care to keep the hands moist—not wet—while the rolling continues.

For building purposes, coils should be even and smooth throughout their length, and about one-third as thick again as the proposed finished wall of the pot. The extra clay is used to weld each coil to the one below, filling the groove between them. It is harder to build a good pot with uneven coils than with perfect ones, and, as there is no limit to the size of pot that can be built by this method, it is worth practising until the art of making coils is perfected.

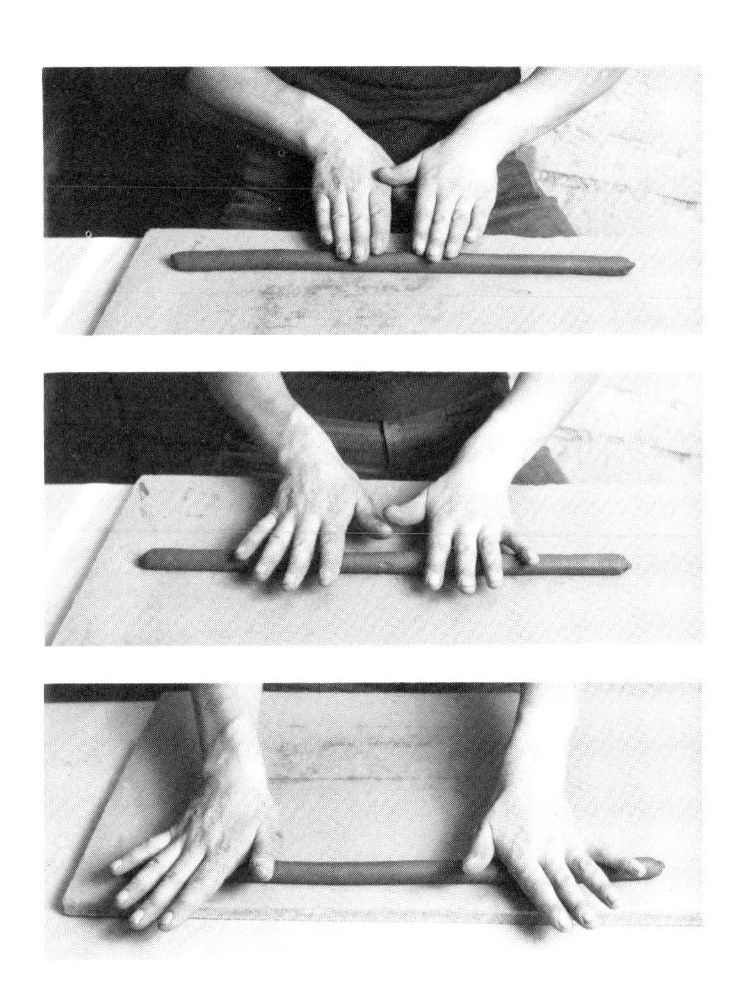

7. Making a coil

To build a pot with coils, first roll out a base the size and shape required. This need not be round; in fact, any shape can be used. It must, however, be even in thickness and smooth on both sides and should contain no air pockets, while the clay should be plastic but not sticky. Place the base on a bat (a piece of porous board), and for ease of working fix the bat to a whirler (see illustration 117) using three lumps of clay.

Place a coil on top of the base so that its outside surface is level with the outer edge of the base. Trim each end to fit, using an oblique cut, and then remove the coil carefully, making sure that it is not stretched. Lightly press the ends together and smooth the join with the fingers. The removal of the coil is most important; if laid on the table, it can be turned over and the join made perfect, ensuring that no air is trapped beneath it on the pot, and at the same time the support of the table ensures that it does not become distorted.

When the coil is properly joined, replace it on the base and press it down gently all round. With one hand, support the outside of the pot; with the thumb or a finger of the other hand, draw down about one-third of the coil on the inside into the groove between it and the base, then smooth it across on to the base a little in order to weld it firmly. When the whole of the coil is joined, smooth out any fingermarks.

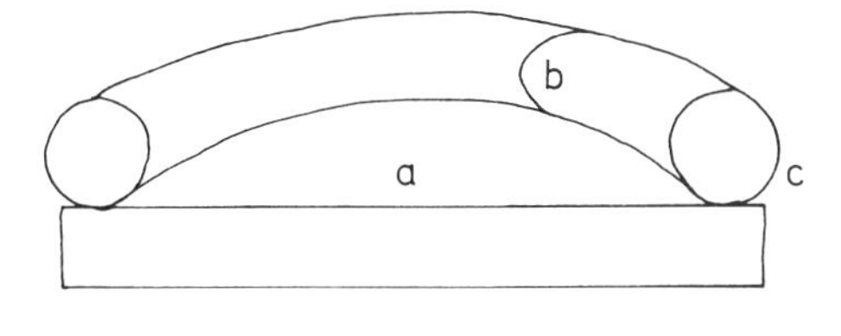

8. Fitting the coil to the base: *a* base; *b* joint; *c* coil position in relation to the edge of the base

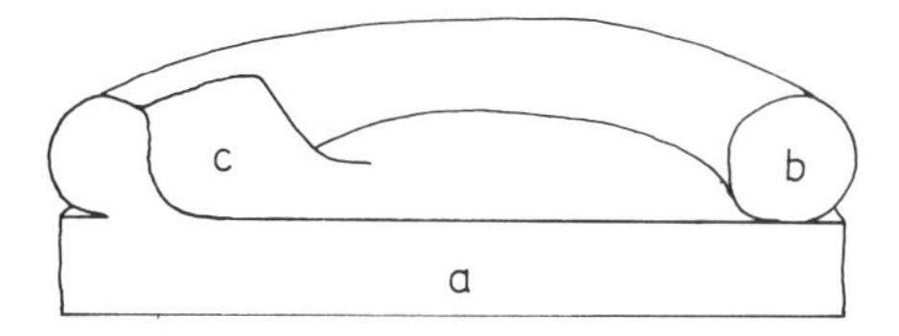

9. Joining the coil on the inside: *a* base; *b* coil pressed gently on to the base; *c* coil pulled down on to the base

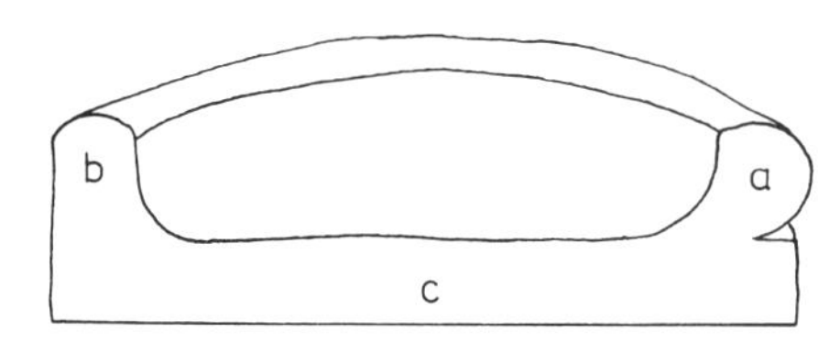

10. The coil joined to the base: *a* inside only; *b* completely joined; *c* base

Now support the inside and work on the outside of the coil. Pull down just enough of the coil with a fingertip to fill in the groove, and smooth it off neatly so that the edge of the base remains neat. If too much is pulled down and the base made uneven, a great deal of tedious tidying up is necessary once the pot has lifted off the bat. This first coil must be joined to the base on the outside of the pot, even if the rest are to be joined only on the inside, to ensure that it does not pull away from the base during drying and firing.

Continue adding coils in this way, fitting each one, removing it to make the join and then welding it to the pot by pulling down sufficient clay to fill the groove and weld it to the coil beneath. As long as the inside is perfectly joined, the outside need not be smoothed over; instead, the coils can be used as part of the external decoration of the pot.

If the pot is to be straight-sided, the coils must be placed squarely on top of one another. To bring the wall inwards, each joined ring should be a little smaller than the previous one, and care must be taken to support the outside of the wall very firmly while welding the inside, in order that the wall shall

11. *Left*: Margaret Mackarness, coiled earthenware oval vase, 24cm. Made at first lesson. *Right*: Ruth Rocket, pentagonal coiled stoneware bottle, 22cm. Part double-dipped

not be pushed outwards. If the walls are to be sloped outwards, each ring must be a little bigger than the last, and again the pressure of the supporting hand must be sufficient to prevent distortion during welding.

The inside of the pot should be smoothed over as the work proceeds; the outside can be left unworked, decorated by tooling or fingering, or smoothed over.

Very delicate work can be done with coils by pinching out each coil after welding it to the pot. This is done by gently squeezing with the thumb and fingers, working round and round the pot until the clay is thinned to the

12. Judy Cunningham-Smith, openwork coiled plant holder, 17cm

desired thickness. But as the height increases, the weight tends to distort the lower regions of the pot. In order to avoid this, after welding each coil on to the thin wall, cover the top 2cm or so of the pot with polythene or a damp rag to keep it workable, then wait until the lower part is hard enough to take the weight of another coil before pinching it out and adding the next ring. Coils can also be added to a thin pinched pot in this way.

The finished pot should be left on the bat to dry out. It will pull away from the bat naturally before the clay becomes unworkable, thus enabling the potter to smooth off any sharp edges created by the action of pulling down the first coil.

Openwork holders for plant pots or candles or purely for decoration can be made using coils. This process takes time and a great deal of patience, as the coils must be supported until they are dry enough to take their own weight and that of any clay above without distorting.

The clay used should be plastic and wet enough for the coils to stick to each other without pressure being applied. Only short lengths of coil about 20cm long should be used, each new one being added when about 5cm of the previous length remains unworked. The join must be made with great care, making sure that it does not show. On the inside of the pot the coils can be smoothed together where they touch to give extra strength. Pieces of plastic foam or screws of soft paper should be used to keep the holes in shape and to support the pot while it dries out. Do not attempt to build too much at once. At the first signs of sagging the work must be left well supported and the top kept damp with a rag or polythene while the lower part dries out enough to take any extra weight.

A suggestion for the use of this method is to include a band of openwork in an otherwise smoothed coil pot.

Building with a continuous coil to produce a random pattern without leaving the gaps to make openwork is another variation. In this case the clay need not be sticky, as the coils can be joined properly on the inside. Make short lengths of coil and add a new one when the previous one is nearly used up, taking care that the join does not show. A glaze which produces good colour runs is very effective on this sort of work, as the colour tends to collect in the grooves, leaving the coil highlighted.

Pinching

Pinching is a good exercise in handling and control of clay. It is, in a way, throwing on a wheel in slow motion. The advantages of the pinching process are that pots can be made square, oval or oblong as well as round; they can be any size, the size and shape of the clay at the start usually determining the final shape and size of the pot (see illustration 13); and, most important,

13. Pinched pots. *Top left*: Ruth Rocket, pot made from a 13lb ball of clay, 17cm. *Top right*: Mollie Herbert, plate, 30cm diameter; Mary Davis, doodles. *Bottom left*: Mollie Herbert, red earthenware bowls, 21cm and 25cm diameter. *Bottom right*: Mollie Herbert, large square pot, raku-fired; Judy Cunningham-Smith, small stoneware vase burnished with oxides, 10cm

bearing in mind our aims of self-sufficiency, they can be made without modern mechanical aids.

It is advisable to make a round bowl for the first attempt at pinching. Start with a piece of clay about 15cm square, cut with a wire from the main block. A plastic but not sticky clay is needed, a red earthenware body being ideal. The clay should be well wedged if it is reconstituted or home-prepared.

Round off the corners by patting the block between the hands, and form it into a spherical shape by rolling it on the work surface with a circular motion, using the palm of the hand. To make the clay even in texture and easy to work, the ball should then be patted gently from hand to hand and rolled between the palms. It is essential that there are no air bubbles in the clay and that the ball is smooth and round.

With three lumps of wet clay, fix a bat to a whirler or a simple saucer-shaped container, and throw the ball of clay on to the centre of the bat so that it sticks firmly. The clay in contact with the bat forms the base of the bowl and it must remain this size, as a weakness develops, leading to cracks in the base, if the walls are pushed or allowed to flop outside this original area.

Next, cup one hand tight against the ball and, keeping it turning with this hand, press the thumb of the other hand down the centre to within 1cm of the bat. Keep the thumb straight so that the top of the hole is not opened

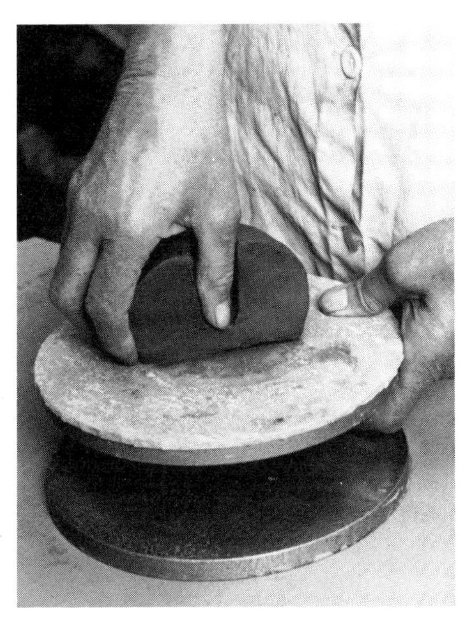

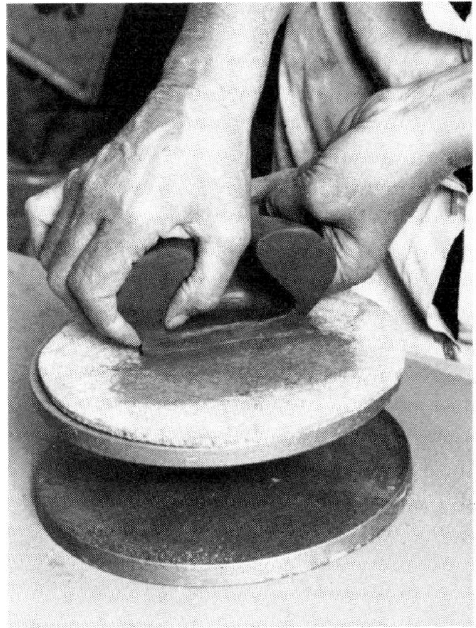

14. Pinching: cross-section, making the hole in the centre of the ball

15. Pinching out the bottom of the wall

16. The walls pinched out to the correct thickness with the rim left thick

out. At the same time, the fingers of this hand pinch gently at the bottom of the ball on the outside to keep it in good shape.

Keeping the supporting hand in position outside, make a circle of the thumb and fingers of the other hand and with the tip of the thumb inside press out against the pads of the fingers round the bottom of the ball until the wall at this level is the required thickness for the finished pot. The thumb should be working a fraction above the fingertips, making a slight upward movement at the same time as the pinch. With the supporting hand, turn the pot a little between every pinch. If there is too much clay to work with the thumb and fingers of one hand, then the index finger should be used inside instead of the thumb, pushing against the supporting hand on the outside.

Continue the pinching, slowly working up the wall and leaving a thick edge at the top. If the pot shows a tendency to flop over the base, it should be supported by means of a screw of newspaper and left until the clay has stiffened enough to take the weight. The paper absorbs moisture from the clay at the weak point while supporting the pot. The rest of the pot should be covered with polythene or a damp rag to ensure that it remains workable.

The shape of the fingers and thumb in relation to each other ensures that the walls develop a natural curve inwards; if the fingers are used on the inside instead of the thumb, the curve will be outwards. Hot dry hands can cause cracks to form in the clay, usually on the outside of the pot; if this occurs keep the hands moist and smooth out the cracks as soon as they appear.

The rim should be finished by working with both hands about 2cm apart on the far side of the work, the pads of the fingers outside pinching against the pads of the thumbs on the inside. With each pinch the hands should be eased towards each other very slightly to prevent the edge from spreading out. Where the edge is uneven in thickness, it can be evened out by pinching the thicker areas each side of a thin place and easing the hands together quite firmly at the same time so that the bumps are pushed sideways to fill up the dips. When the rim is neat and even it can be finished off by smoothing it with a piece of wet leather.

A more globular shape can be produced by making a slight upward movement of the fingers on the outside with every pinch; when finishing the rim the fingers should pull the clay inwards over the pads of the thumbs, and the easing together of the hands should be more pronounced.

To make a dish, the same process should be followed as for the bowl, until the first 2 or 3cm of the wall have been pinched out; the pinching should then be done with the thumb on the outside of the pot and the fingers on the inside, working on the side of the pot nearest to the body. This should be done very slowly and gently so as to avoid stretching and cracking the clay. If a large dish is being made, the underside should be supported with screws of newspaper if it shows signs of sagging, and it must be supported in this way while drying to prevent warping and strain.

Coils can be added to pinched pots. This is done by allowing the walls to dry out enough to take the extra weight while keeping the rim thick and damp enough to take the coils. Quite large pots can be made by adding coils in this way and pinching them out to the thickness of the rest of the pot.

A small pinched pot, or thumb pot as it is sometimes called, can be made by cupping a small ball of clay in one hand and working with the other hand. The important point to remember is that, once the initial hole is made, the thumb must be kept bent while pinching out against the fingers, so that a thick roll of clay is left on the rim of the work. This thick edge can be worked out to form a very fine rim once the rest of the pot has stiffened up. Very delicate light pots can be made in this way.

It is important to have an even thickness of clay throughout the pinched pot, whatever its size. If the middle of the base is left very thick and its edges and the walls are thin, the thin parts will dry more quickly; as they shrink they will set up tensions which will probably cause the base to split. If there is any doubt as to whether a pot is even in thickness, it is best to cut it carefully in half with a wire. The section should be like that shown in illustration 17. If it is correct, the clay can be wedged up and another pot made with the knowledge that the first one was good. If it is uneven, then the different thicknesses should be felt very carefully so that when the next attempt is made it will be possible to gauge more accurately just how thick the walls and base are.

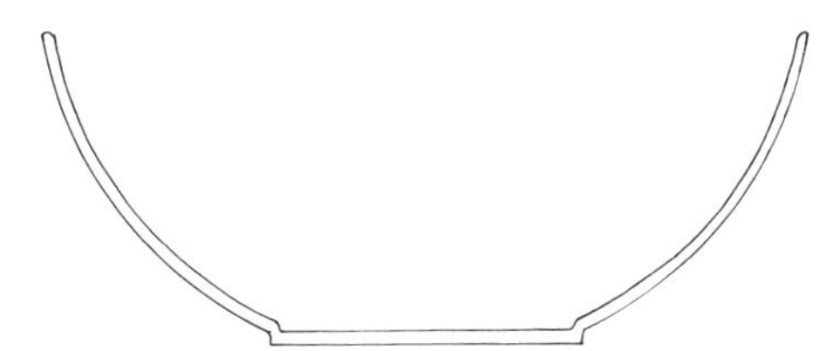

17. Cross-section showing a finished pinched pot

If the rim of a pinched pot is very uneven in height, it can be levelled off by marking it with a needle, held very firmly, with the hand resting on a stable support at the correct height. The spare clay can then be cut off and the rim smoothed with a piece of wet leather.

The inside of a pinched pot should be quite smooth. This can be achieved by using a scraper (see illustration 35), the fingers or even a pebble. The outside, on the other hand, can be left with the fingermarks showing, as this can produce a very attractive effect, especially if a glaze producing marked colour runs is used. Alternatively, the outside can be burnished and left unglazed, and after firing it can be waxed and polished in the same way as wood. Other methods of finishing and decorating are described in Chapter 4.

Pinching angular shapes is an alternative to building with slabs of clay. The advantage is that the corners have no joins and can be made very smooth and rounded, an important point when making dishes to contain food.

Work a piece of clay into a smooth lump with no cracks or air pockets. The base must be the shape and size required for the finished article. The prepared lump for a simple butter dish would be about 2cm thick, 13cm long and 7cm wide, with the corners neatly rounded.

Fix the prepared lump to a bat and, using the thumb, press a groove along the centre of it, leaving a 5mm base and an even thickness of wall all round the sides.

With one hand supporting the clay and turning the work as necessary, use the tip of the other thumb inside the pot to press out the lower edge of the wall against the support of the fingers of this same hand on the outside, squeezing up a thick edge all round.

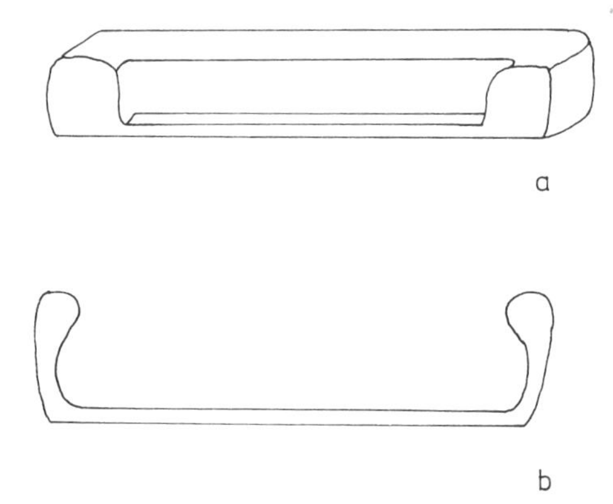

18. Pinching a butter dish: *a* the centre groove; *b* the walls pinched out and the rim left thick

Change to using the pads of the thumbs and fingers of both hands, working about 2cm apart, and pinch the edge to the required thickness. With each pinch ease the hands together to prevent the edge from spreading out and becoming frilly. When the walls are of the correct thickness the rim should, if necessary, be trimmed to an even height and smoothed off with a piece of wet leather. The inside of the dish should be made perfectly smooth using the fingers or a scraper.

Quite large, square pots can be produced by pinching. Starting with a prepared square block of clay and always supporting the outside with one hand, make a square hole in the centre of the lump; this can be done using thumb, fingers or a square block of wood, depending on the size of the lump of clay. Once the hole is made, pinch the walls in the same manner as described for the making of a round pot, but take care to keep the corners shaped as they will round up naturally if allowed to. The larger of the two pots shown in illustration 13, bottom right, was pinched from a 7lb lump of clay; the outside was left uneven and the corners exaggerated to enhance the effect of raku reduction firing (see Glossary).

Slab Work

Slab work is familiarly known as 'pastry-making' among our students because the clay is rolled out with a rolling pin in much the same way as pastry; and, as with the production of good pastry, the preparation and rolling out is the most important part of the operation. From the method of using the slabs, it could just as well be referred to as 'joinery'.

Building with slabs is a versatile process with plenty of scope for imagination. Some examples of this are shown in illustrations 19 and 22.

19. Christine Upton, sculpting-marl slab wheels, 25cm and 14cm diameter; Mary Mack, stoneware slab box

There are some important points which should be borne in mind when using slabs:

1. The body used should be a strong, well grogged or sanded clay to reduce the possibility of warping.
2. Care should be taken to ensure that there are no air pockets within the slabs.
3. Slabs should be of even thickness, because otherwise uneven shrinkage during drying and firing causes stresses which distort or crack the pot. For the same reason, the moisture content should not differ from slab to slab.
4. The slip (slurry) used to make the joints must be made from the same clay as the slabs and should be wet and sticky but not runny.
5. All joints must be well made and free of air pockets.
6. When building on to a base, the side slabs must be fitted to the top of the base and not round the sides.

The following articles are needed when rolling out clay: a sheet of smooth absorbent board; a clean dry rolling pin; two strips of wood the thickness of the slabs required, to act as guides for the rolling pin; and, if a textured surface is desired, a small amount of grog or sand, or a piece of cloth or sacking. If the slabs are to be kept smooth and untextured, the clay must be dry enough not to stick to the board or rolling pin.

Having collected all the necessary articles, take a slice of clay and, with the guides in place on the board, gently beat it out with the rolling pin, turning it over and round through 90° so that the clay is spread evenly in all directions. Do this until it is still twice the thickness of the guides. This beating is quicker than trying to roll out right from the start, and it helps to remove any small air bubbles which may be present; furthermore, rolling tends to stretch the clay, so the less done the better.

The clay can now be rolled out to the required thickness. Continue occasionally to turn it over and round. Too heavy a pressure will cause the clay to crack on the underside; patience and light rolling is better than hasty heavy action.

Keep the rolling pin completely clean, as any adhering clay will mark the slab. If the clay begins to stick to the working surface or rolling pin, and sand or grog is not being used, turn the board over or change to a dry board and rolling pin. If sand or grog is being used to provide a textured surface, then the board and pin may be dusted with it in the same way as flour is used in pastry-making.

If an air bubble appears, prick it carefully, squeeze the air out and smooth the clay over again.

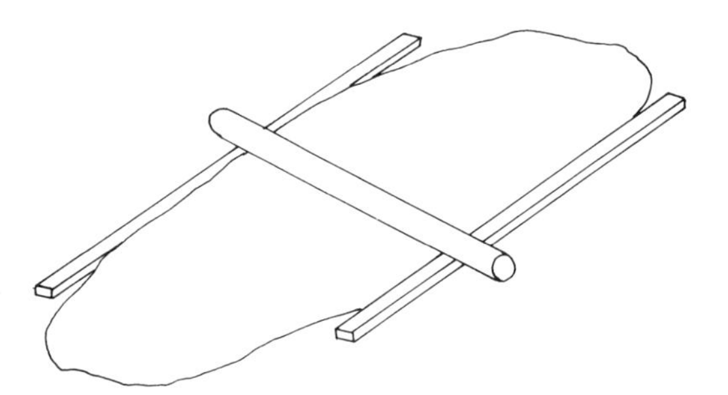

20. Rolling out clay using batten guides

The easiest way to learn the technique of building with slabs is to make an open-topped box. To do this, first cut a cardboard or stiff paper pattern of the size and shape required—allowing for the shrinkage of the clay when it is fired. The walls should be cut to fit together as shown in illustration 21, *a* or *b*.

Place the pattern on the clay; then, with a ruler or straight-edge on top to hold it firmly, cut round it with a thin blade or palette knife. An ordinary knife will tend to pull and distort the clay.

Leave the slabs on the board until they are leather-hard (stiff and dry-feeling but still pliable), turning them occasionally to ensure even drying. This is best done by placing a clean board on top of them and turning the two boards with the slabs between them, thus enabling the wet board to be removed and the slabs turned without distortion.

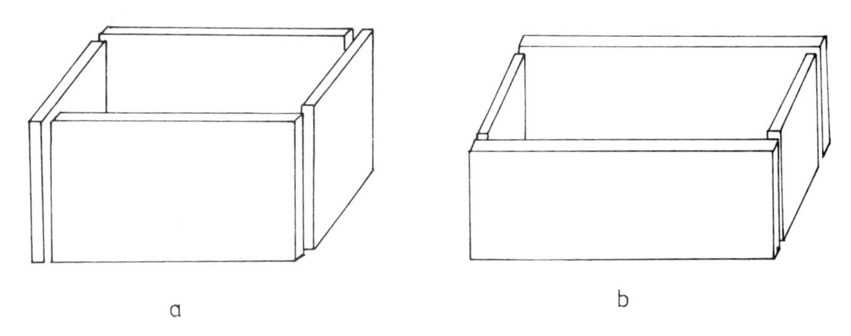

21. Assembly of slabs for making a box

When the slabs are firm enough to stand on their own without bending, work out the order in which they are to be assembled, remembering that, if the assembly is as shown in illustration 21*b*, then the last slab to be added must be one of the outer ones, as it is very awkward to fit a slab accurately between two walls already in place.

Working one slab at a time, cross-score the edges to be joined, using a piece of hacksaw blade or comb, and dab slip on to one of the scored surfaces of each joint. The slip is better applied too thick than too thin. The excess will ooze out and can be wiped off carefully.

As soon as the slip is applied, place the slab in position. Holding it between the palms of the hands, press the edges together slightly to squeeze out any excess slip and then, still supporting it, wriggle it slightly until it can be felt to grip in the same way as a rubber sucker pressed on to a pane of glass. Wipe off any spare slip and prop the slab if necessary while the next one is being prepared.

A thin coil of clay can be worked into the joints on the inside to strengthen and neaten them. This is something which should be done to any slab-built pot that is to be used for food or drink.

There is no excuse for not finishing a pot well. Unless they are a deliberate feature of the work, all rough edges should be smoothed off, either by tooling when wet, or with a ball of sisal fibre—teased-out twine—when dry. A ragged edge does not take glaze well. Particular attention should be given to the base of a pot, as a rough bottom can ruin any surface on which it is placed. The inside of a pot should be as neatly finished as the outside. Apart from the satisfaction that can be obtained from perfection in one's work, there is the matter of hygiene to be considered when making pots for food and water. The pot with unfinished surfaces cannot easily be cleaned.

The above is the basis of slab work. The principles of building are the same if wet instead of leather-hard slabs are to be used. In this case the slabs can be shaped and supported in the chosen shape as they dry, thus introducing curves into an otherwise angular structure.

Work can be done to a plan or at random; the possibilities are almost limitless. The only restrictions are that the slabs and the slip must be made from the same clay, and that the slabs must all have the same moisture content.

Pin pots—so-called because they are usually formed round a rolling pin—are made from wet slabs. They can just as well be shaped round any smooth, flat-bottomed, straight-sided object, such as a block of wood, a bottle or a section of pipe with one end plugged. They can be square, oval, round or polyhedral. This is an excellent way to make mugs or jugs.

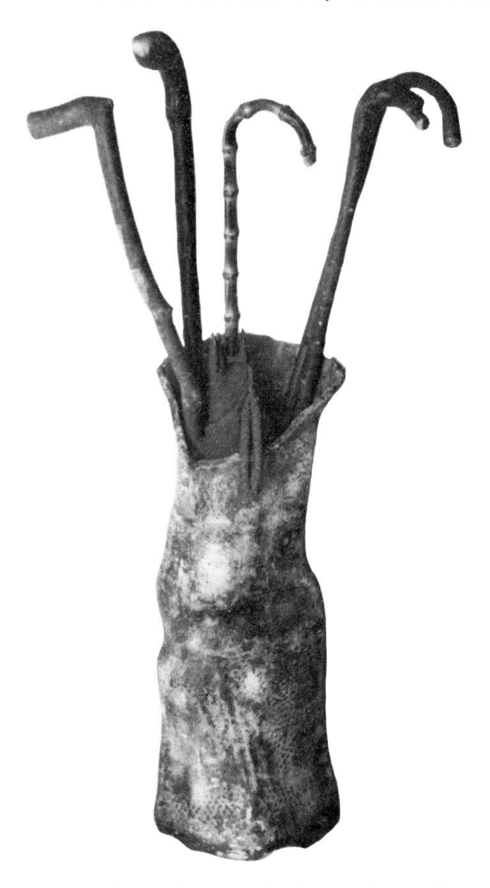

22. Mollie Herbert, umbrella stand. Random construction of stoneware slabs, 58cm

Wrap a sheet of paper from a magazine round the mould and secure the edges with sticky tape. This is to prevent the clay from sticking to the mould.

Roll out the clay to the thickness required; cut out a base, making it about 1cm bigger than necessary, and place it on a bat.

To make the wall of the pot, the slab should be cut as shown in illustration 23. Place the mould with the bottom level with edge *a*, then roll the clay carefully on to the mould until cut edge *b* meets the uncut slab. Taking care not to distort it, lightly mark the clay where the edge meets the slab. Gently unroll it and, using a straight-edge, cut the second edge *c* obliquely to fit the first one so that when the two are joined they form an overlapping joint.

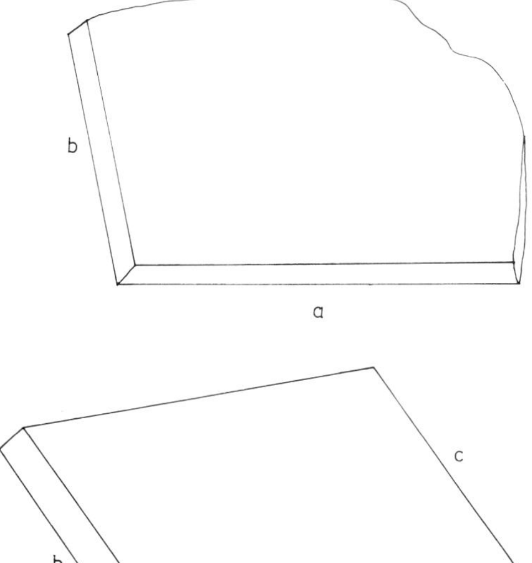

23. Slab cut ready for fitting to a mould

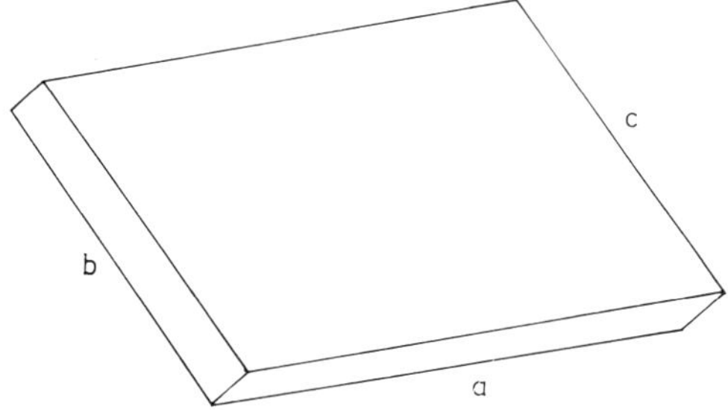

24. Slab cut to size and shape ready for assembly round a mould

Score both edges and apply slip to one. Wrap the slab around the mould and gently wriggle the edges together as in joining straight slabs, remembering that too much pressure on the soft clay will cause marking which can only be remedied by starting again. Wipe off any excess slip and, by smoothing very gently, remove all traces of the joint. A good tool for this purpose is a palette knife. The tube is now ready to be joined to the base.

With the mould still in place, stand the clay tube on the base and mark lightly round the edge. Remove the tube and score the bottom edge and the base, taking care not to score the base inside the thickness of the tube. Apply plenty of slip and press the tube gently into place, wriggling it as before until it can be felt to grip. Clean off any surplus slip and if required trim the base, using a thin blade and making many small cuts rather than trying to cut

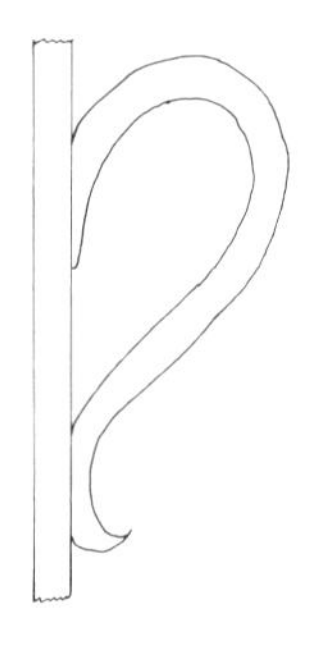

25. Recommended method of attaching a handle to a pin pot

round in one sweep. The join can then be smoothed over with a palette knife, using upward strokes so that the base remains true.

The top edge should be trimmed with the mould in place, and if a handle is to be applied this should be done before the mould is removed.

It is more in keeping with the nature of the pin pot to use a handle made from a strip of rolled-out clay than one that has been made from a coil or pulled. Handles should be fixed by the standard technique of scoring, applying slip and wriggling into place until the joint is firm. The upper end of a handle is best applied with the end turned over and pointing downwards, as this gives the strongest anchorage. It is advisable to bind handles with damp rag or polythene while the rest of the pot dries off; otherwise the handle will dry faster than the main body of the pot, and may very well pull away or crack.

26. Pin pots. *Left to right*: Mary Davis, carved stoneware; Judy Cunningham-Smith, earthenware pencil pin pots, and earthenware pin pot shaped and carved after the mould was removed, 20cm; Mollie Herbert, textured earthenware, double-dipped

As soon as the clay has stiffened up enough to stand on its own, the mould should be removed by sliding it out, leaving the paper behind. The paper is removed by twisting it slowly to pull it away from the clay, as opposed to trying to slide it out in the same manner as the mould. The mould must be taken out as soon as possible; if it is left in place, the pot will split as it dries and contracts.

The inside of the joints should be cleaned up and smoothed over, using a long smooth piece of wood or a sponge on the end of a stick.

This method of making pots is quite versatile. Several pots can be built on to the same base, or a number of separate pots joined together. Tubes of differing shapes and sizes can be built up at random. Very small tubes can be made round pencils or knitting needles.

Doodles

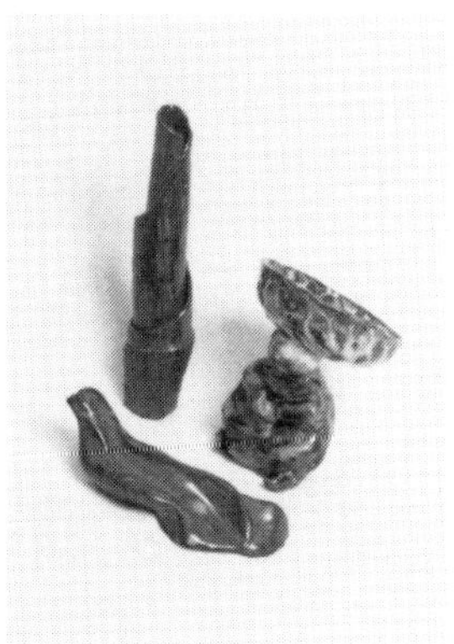

27. Doodles and unwinds. *Top left:* Denise Bates; Andrea Cunningham, 'legs', 35cm; Mary Mack. *Top right*: Judy Cunningham-Smith; Lill Butcher; Mollie Herbert. *Bottom left*: Andrea Cunningham, clay spiral, 22cm; Wyn Dart, Mexican, 15cm; Mary Mack, 'seal'. *Bottom right*: Betty Stoy, pillar, 28cm; Bridget Jolliffe

Most students at one time or another reach a stage where they start trying too hard. This can be for any number of reasons, but the result is the same—their work suffers and nothing seems to come out right. When this happens we get them to 'unwind' by taking a piece of clay and simply doodling, with no idea of making anything definite. This can produce amazing results; the students relax and often make something quite unrelated to their usual work.

Generally, the methods used are carving into a solid block, squeezing and moulding a piece of soft clay in the hands, and building up at random using coils or strips. This can lead to the discovery of a hitherto hidden talent for modelling.

After 'unwinding' in this way, the potter seems to have far more confidence and approaches work with fresh ideas. We ourselves are incurable doodlers, finding it very relaxing after teaching the same thing for several classes in a row.

Illustration 27 shows a selection of unwinds made by these methods.

3 Adaptations of Traditional Primitive Methods of Construction

The indigenous inhabitants of many regions, including Africa, North and South America, the Caribbean and Fiji, can teach us much of self-sufficiency in pottery-making, as most use only locally dug clays and readily available fuels for firing in the open air.

The modern potter cannot expect to attain quickly the high standards achieved by these people with their generations of inherited skills and traditions, but we have studied many of their methods and adapted them to suit the abilities, climates and traditions of the modern world. We feel proud if we can build and fire a pot or sculpture which has something of the beautiful simplicity produced by the people of these ancient cultures.

28. Mollie Herbert, coiled and thinned urn, made from mixed brick clay and sculpting marl, burnished and painted with oxides for firing in the updraft kiln, 25cm

'Primitive' in the context of this book does not mean crude. In fact, the methods of construction used by these cultures are often highly developed. Every pot or sculpture should be finished well, the beauty of perfection in simplicity often far outweighing that of the complex. It is possible to produce by primitive methods work which has more character and gives more satisfaction to the potter than anything made by the more modern methods of slip casting and throwing.

The polished surfaces of a finished creation, showing the warmth of the clay and the variation of colour caused by partial reduction (see p. 50), produce a pleasing effect of natural simplicity. Pots with black 'flashes', caused by the depositing of carbon in the clay during firing, are much prized and sought after by some African tribes.

Beating

In northern Nigeria the Adarawa Hausa men beat out large water pots with a dry clay pestle. Beating on the inside only, they work with a large lump of clay in a mould (which can be a hollow in the ground or part of a calabash), turning the pot continually as they beat out the walls against the mould. We believe that a method similar to the one described below is employed by potters in Tibet, who use wooden beaters, but we have not yet heard of stones being used in the same way.

The following method we have worked out for ourselves; we find it very hard work but extremely rewarding. It follows the same principles as pinching, but stones are used instead of fingers, and the pot is kept turning slowly, either on a bat fixed to a whirler or on the simple equivalent—a saucer-shaped container, preferably made from low-fired clay, placed so that

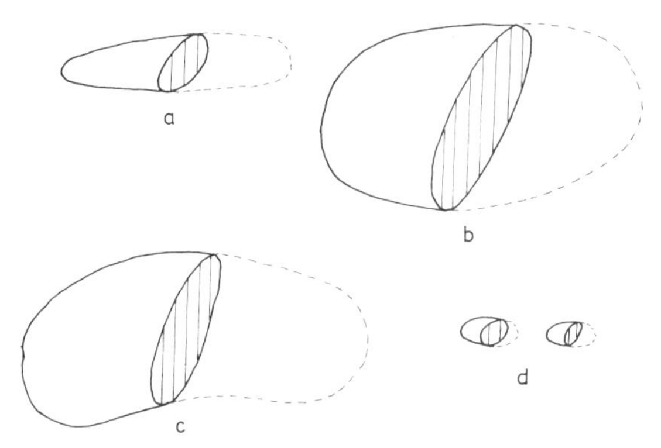

29. Stones suitable for beating: *a* long, for starting; *b* inside beater; *c* outside beater; *d* pebbles for finishing the rim and burnishing

it can be turned with ease while the pot is worked on. It is best to work in a drying atmosphere, for example in the sun or in a warm room, and to stand or kneel over the work.

Choose water-worn stones which are comfortable to handle: a long round one, or a stick with a rounded end, to start the inside, an oval one to beat on the inside of the pot and a flattish curved one for the outside. Rough stones such as pumice or broken concrete used on the outside can give a very interesting finish to the work.

Quite large pots can be made by this method of beating, as the action of the stones helps to consolidate and dry the clay as work proceeds, thus avoiding collapse of the walls. The stones must be kept clean, any clay adhering to them being rubbed off immediately.

Work the clay into a ball with a smooth round base and place it on the bat or saucer. With the long stone or stick, pound a hole in the centre of the ball, leaving 1cm of clay for the base. This hole needs to be fairly large to make room to beat the stone against the inner walls.

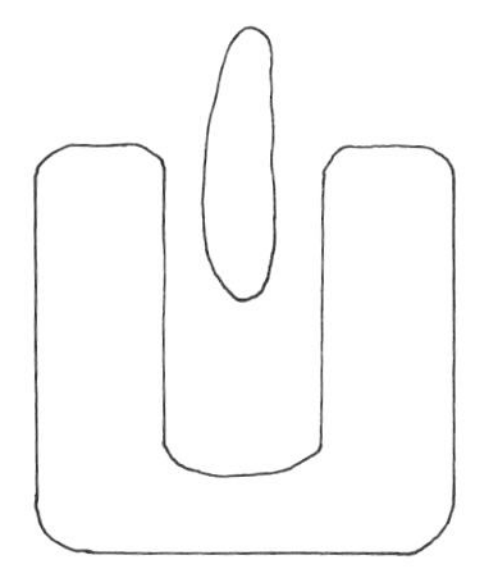

30. Beating: making the centre hole

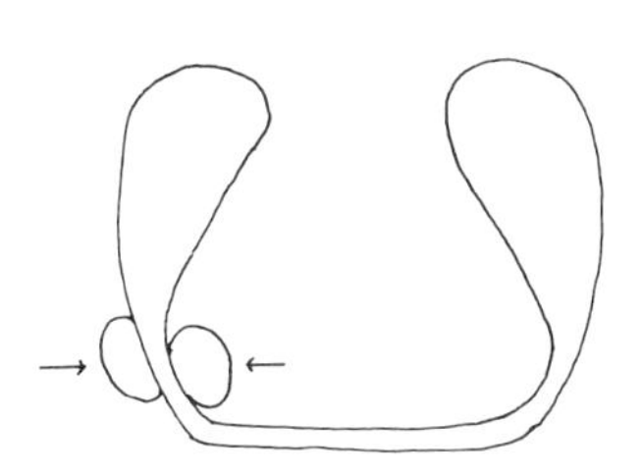

31. Beating out the walls

Change to the oval stone inside and the flat one outside. Then start at the bottom of the wall and, using a regular rhythm, beat the stones towards each other, at the same time pulling slightly to make the pot turn a little with each stroke. Gradually work up the wall, shaping as desired, with the inner stone slightly higher than the outer one if the wall is to be curved outwards, the outer one higher than the inner if it is to be brought inwards.

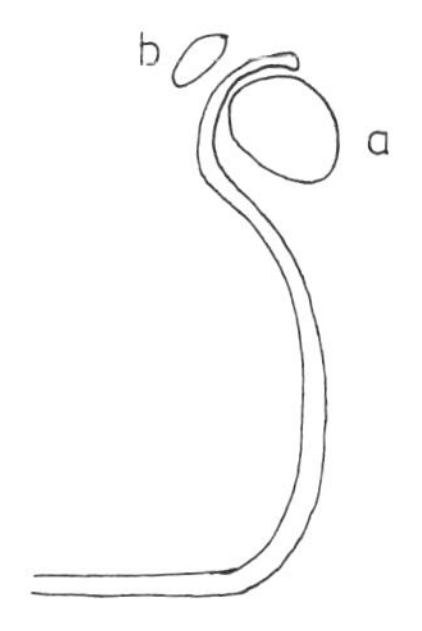

32. Shaping the rim: *a* support; *b* small flat pebble to work the clay

The walls can be beaten to the required thickness in one operation, or, if the clay is a bit too soft, they can be left thicker and the beating process repeated when they are dry enough to support their own weight.

The inside of the pot can be scraped smooth with a pebble or kidney-shaped tool. The outside can be left with the stone-marks showing, or alternatively can be smoothed and burnished. Iron oxides or wood ash can be burnished into the walls at this stage. It is interesting to try to finish a pot using only stones; in this case the rim can be beaten gently into shape, leaving the slightly wavy edge made by the stones, or smoothed off neatly using a small flat pebble.

The decoration best suited to this type of pot is that done by impression or appliqué as described in Chapter 4.

33. Pam Teggin, beaten earthenware pot, 15cm

Pulling

Pulling is a fascinating process used by some Africans to make large water vessels and cooking pots. Since we introduced this method into our teaching, a number of students have become 'hooked' on it and many pots are being produced which look happy to be alive.

It is best to work in the open air on a hot dry day, or in the pottery workshop when it is warm and dry from firing the kiln.

It is essential that the body used is of the correct texture and moisture content. Heavily grogged bodies as available from most suppliers are suitable for this type of work. The moisture content is best gauged through trial and error, as the temperature and humidity of the air determines how quickly the pot will dry out during the process of pulling up the walls. If it is too wet and the air cannot dry it quickly enough, the pot will be uncontrollable and will flop out of shape. Very thin, light pots can be made using a fine body with up to 45 per cent of fine filler mixed into it.

34. Pulled pots. *Left*: John Millest, red earthenware with silica sand filler. *Centre*: Jane Jackson. *Right*: Janet Cunningham, red earthenware with granite-dust filler, 21cm

It is best to stand or kneel over the work to make a pulled pot. Form the clay into a cylindrical shape with a diameter equal to the size of the base required for the finished pot. Place it on a bat fixed to a whirler, or on the simple equivalent, and, working gradually down the centre, scoop fingersful of clay up and on to the top of the walls, thus building the walls up and hollowing out the inside of the pot. At this stage the wall should remain straight. The other hand should be used to support the outside and to turn the pot a little between each pull. Continue to scoop out the centre until the walls are 2.5-3cm thick, occasionally smoothing the clay into the rim.

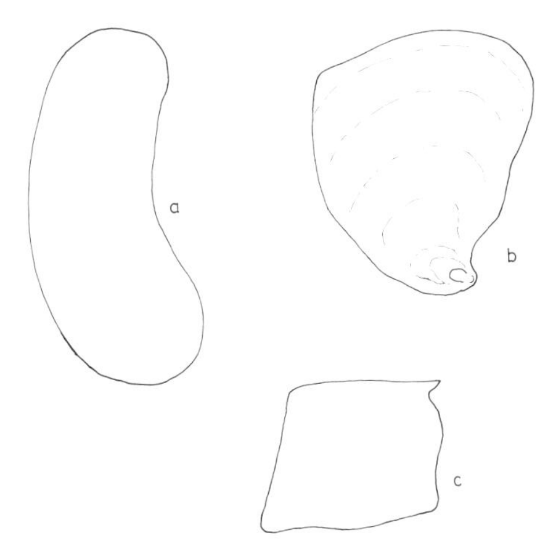

35. Tools for pulling: *a* wooden kidney-shaped scraper; *b* oyster shell; *c* chamois leather

36. Pulling up on the inside. The walls are beginning to shape to the supporting hand

Another method is to pull the clay up on the outside as well as the inside, using both hands at once. The most suitable method for each individual can only be discovered through trial and error. Climate, the body used, the abilities of the potter, the size of the hands and the length of the fingers are all determining factors. We made many attempts before developing the techniques to suit ourselves.

The next step is to smooth and shape the walls by drawing clay up, using a curved shell or a kidney-shaped wooden scraper. Supporting the outside with the palm of the hand and always working against this support, draw up the spare clay from the inside, starting at the base and making the full sweep to the rim. If the full sweep is not performed, ridges will form in the wall. The spare clay is still added to the rim and shaped to the pot. The scraping of the inside starts to shape the pot against the supporting hand on the outside of the wall, and the weight of the clay causes the wall to sag into a natural curve. This combination of factors produces a shape particular to the individual potter, which is why an African can produce many hundreds of hand-pulled pots which are to all intents and purposes identical in shape. It is in fact very difficult to break away from this personal shape to any appreciable degree.

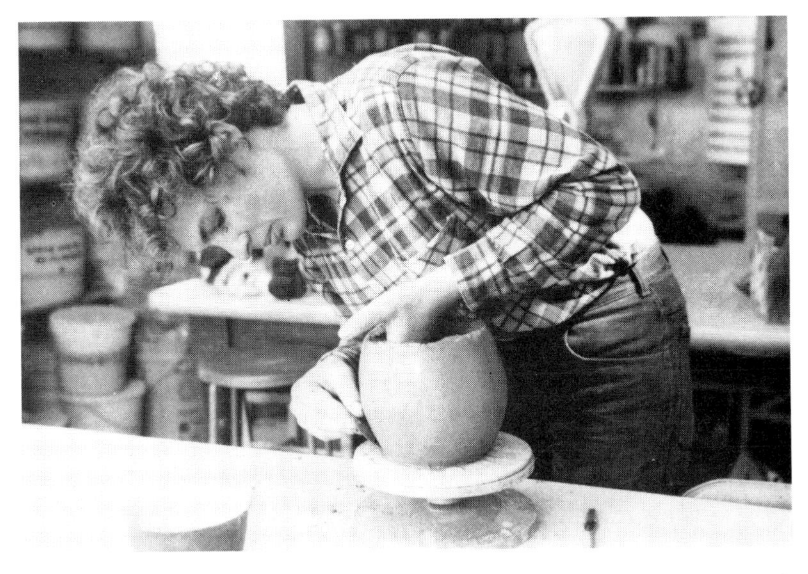

37. Smoothing the outside, welding in the clay brought up to the rim, using a kidney scraper

38. Adding a coil on to the rim of a pulled pot

When the inside is smooth, start on the outside with a hand inside for support. The rim should be shaped at this stage. The opening can be narrowed to a very great extent by using spare clay removed from the outside, or by adding on sausages of clay which should be smoothed out and welded on to the pot with the scraper. The thickness of the walls can be reduced to as little as 3mm if the body is fine enough in texture. The rim can be smoothed and made even by turning the pot steadily—or moving round the pot if it is particularly large—while holding a piece of soft wet leather or a shiny leaf folded over it.

If the walls are particularly thin, and especially if the pot is to be fired in a bush firing, the rim should be left thicker than the walls; this strengthens the pot, and it is less likely to be chipped.

If the pot is to be bush-fired, it should be burnished on the inside when it is leather-hard and either burnished or otherwise decorated on the outside. There is no reason why a pulled pot should not be decorated and fired in a modern kiln like any other pot.

39. Burnishing, using a thumbnail

Building with Lumps and Sausages

Although mechanisation is gradually taking over in the Caribbean islands to cope with tourist demand, some potters still use the traditional methods. They build up their pots very quickly, using lumps of wet, coarse-textured clay, smoothing out each lump as it is applied. In the intense dry heat of the islands the pots dry out very rapidly as they are built, enabling them to keep their shape well. They are baked out in the open in a simple wood and grass fire. The charcoal-burning stove known as a 'coal pot', shown in illustration 40, was recently made by this method on the island of Antigua.

40. Mrs Graham, Antigua, Caribbean 'coal pot' cooking stove

This method of building can be used by potters in this country if they work with a heavily grogged body, such as Fulham Pottery sculpting marl or Podmore's raku body, which both contain 40 per cent of coarse grog. Prepared clay from the suppliers is not normally wet enough for this purpose, in which case each lump should be dipped briefly into a bowl of water just before applying it to the pot.

It is not necessary to use a whirler. Form a base on a bat and add small lumps to it to build up the shape required. Weld each bit on to the pot by smoothing it with the fingers or a scraper before adding the next bit. If the walls begin to sag because they are not drying fast enough, the edges should be covered and the pot left until it is stiff enough to continue.

This method of building tends to produce a thick-walled pot ideal for heavy articles such as umbrella stands and large plant tubs. Solid sculptures can be built up without fear of breakages during firing, because the shrinkage of such a heavily grogged body is very slight.

41. Dianne Farrant, sculpting-marl urn pre-fired in the electric kiln before bush firing, 27cm

The walls of a pot made in this way can be thinned down in the same manner as those of a pulled pot, but owing to the coarseness of the grog the limit is about 5mm. If a thin pot is required, it is better to use a finer body and either beat or pull it.

A variation of this method is to use short sausages of soft clay. A way of making very large pots without having to cope with a vast lump of clay right from the start is to make the bottom part of the pot by beating or pulling and then to continue building up the walls by the addition of sausages. Many of the Africans do this, and we find it very satisfactory as long as the pot can be dried out rapidly while it is being made. Otherwise, it has to be left to stiffen before adding each ring of sausages, which makes it a long and tedious process.

The body used should contain a filler which need not necessarily be coarse, as each sausage is thinned out in the process of welding it to the rim. The body should be wet and sticky but able to hold its shape well.

Each sausage should be no longer than twice the width of the hand, otherwise it will be impossible to control while working it on to the pot. Its diameter should be such that it can be easily held in the hand.

Hold the sausage in one hand and, using the other hand as a support for the outside, apply the sausage to the pot by squashing the end on to the inside of the rim with the thumb. Then, feeding the sausage through the hand, continue to squash the rest of it on to the rim. To avoid unevenness in height, a complete circle of sausages should be added before they are smoothed out. The pot is shaped either by scraping with a wooden tool or by using the fingers in the manner described for pulling pots. The surface of the finished pot can be decorated in any manner suited to its shape and weight.

Pots made by any of these methods of construction can of course be fired and glazed like any other pottery.

42. Bridget Jolliffe, sculpting-marl bottle built up using lumps and sausages. Dribbled glaze over a base glaze, 28cm

4 Decoration of Unfired Clay

Decoration of pottery is a matter for the individual potter, who should strive for personal satisfaction. It should also be governed by the design of the pot. It is impossible to create something which pleases everyone, so it is best to start by pleasing oneself; if the result pleases others too, that is an added satisfaction. Work done to suit another's tastes is not truly one's own work. In

43. Burnished bush-fired pots, waxed after firing. *Top left*: Mollie Herbert, jar, coiled and pinched out, burnished with manganese oxide, 21cm. *Top right*: Janet Cunningham, coiled sculpting-marl jug painted with crocus martis, 26cm. *Bottom left*: Mollie Herbert, coiled brick-marl bottle, 11cm; Christine Upton, coiled jar with impressed decoration painted with iron oxides, 30cm; Denise Bates, doodle. *Bottom right*: Beryl Watts, dinosaur, carbonised sculpting marl; Jean Barnes, head, 17cm; Andrea Cunningham, dog

such a personal matter it is difficult to give any definite instructions, but there are a number of basic methods of decoration which we teach and which can be combined and adapted to suit the wishes of the individual.

Burnishing

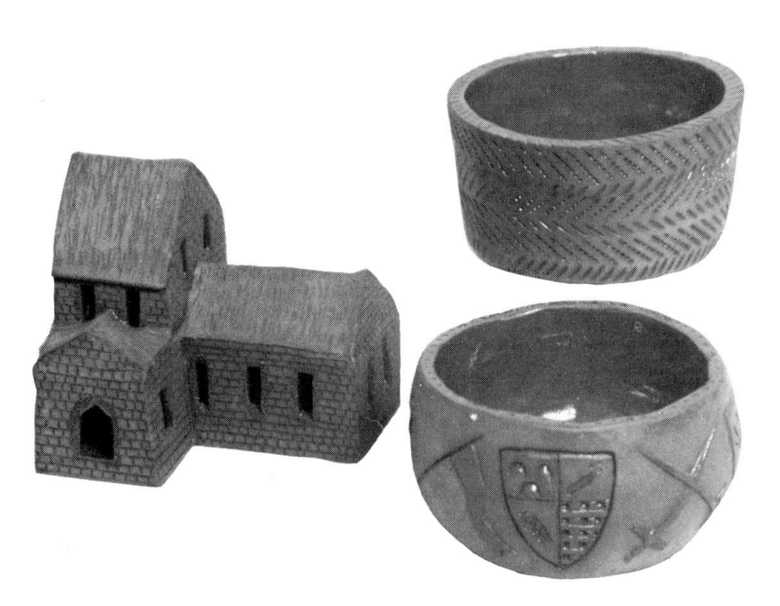

44. Red earthenware with transparent glaze wiped off to leave the glaze in the patterns. *Left*: Jean Newton, church, 12.5cm. *Top right*: Flo Rudd. *Bottom right*: Denise Bates

Most of the traditional African potters, who do not use glazes, usually finish their work by burnishing, which is polishing the leather-hard clay. The compacting effect of the rubbing strengthens the pot and can give an almost watertight finish. Pots finished in this way are used for cooking and as water containers and storage jars.

Any pot or model can be burnished, regardless of the clay used, and any method of firing is possible (see illustration 43). After firing, the burnished ware can be wax-polished if it is not to be used for food or water, or, while it is still hot from the firing, can be dipped into a hot tannin solution (see instructions for bush firing). Burnished ware which is to be fired in a modern kiln can be glazed on the inside to make it watertight while still having the waxed exterior. Without the glazed interior the gradual evaporation of water through the walls will form a bloom on the wax.

The tools used for burnishing are a matter of personal preference. The back of a spoon, a water-worn stone, a fingernail or any part of the hand which will give a polish to the clay are all suitable. Some Africans use a string of hard round seeds, a tough shiny leaf or a piece of soft leather. The work should be leather-hard—that is, the clay should not stick to the finger when it is rubbed.

Work systematically round the pot, using a gentle circular motion, and continue rubbing until a high degree of polish is obtained. If the surface gets too dry and starts to powder before satisfactory results are achieved, dampen a section at a time with a little spittle and polish it with the fingers. Spittle is far more effective for this purpose than water, which tends to make the surface lose its polish.

Pleasing effects can be obtained by rubbing raw powdered oxides into the surface before burnishing, especially if the pot is to be fired in a reducing atmosphere such as an updraft kiln or bush fire.

Reduction can only occur in a kiln heated by flames, thus it cannot normally take place in an electric one. It occurs when all available oxygen in the air has been burnt. The fire then draws on the oxygen atoms combined within the oxides in the pottery being fired. This in effect 'reduces' the oxides, in some cases to the extent that only the pure metal remains. The opposite, oxidation, occurs where there is ample oxygen within the kiln and no fire to consume it.

Reduction can be achieved in an electric kiln by introducing substances such as wood or naphthalene (mothballs) when the kiln has reached firing temperature, but this does great harm to the elements. However, it can be effected without damage to the elements by sealing the pots to be reduced within an unglazed container (saggar) together with a piece of pitch-pine or naphthalene.

Impressing

The African potters are masters of this art, which gives a bold, individual appearance to the finished pot (see illustration 45). The traditional tools of the Africans are carved wooden roulettes, sharp bamboo slivers and coarse twine, but any hard object which will make a pleasing pattern in the clay is suitable. Roulettes and stamps can be made by carving leather-hard clay and firing it to produce durable tools which are personal to the potter who made them.

Making sure the wall is supported on the other side, the tool is pressed cleanly into the clay so as to leave no ragged edges. If a scratching motion is used, the lines are not smooth-edged because the clay is dragged by the tool. In the case of a roulette or twine a rolling action is used.

Impressed decoration on a burnished pot can be greatly enhanced by applying glaze and then sponging it off the surface, leaving the glaze in the decoration. This can be taken a stage further by using a dark glaze and then applying a transparent glaze over the top. The latter method is equally effective where the pot has not been burnished.

45. Lill Butcher, coiled brick-clay jar with impressed decoration. Burnished with iron oxides, 20cm. Fired in the updraft kiln Mk 1

Carving

To carve clay, it is essential to have tools which are sharp and clean. The clay should be firm and damp. If it is dry it will chip.

The design can be drawn on to the clay very lightly, to provide a guide, and the clay cut away using any suitable tool.

Etching can be done with a fine tool such as those used by dentists. The pair of pots shown in illustration 46 were burnished before etching and afterwards dipped into a dark blue transparent glaze which was then sponged off, leaving the design picked out in blue. After firing they were waxed to give the effect of polished wood.

For carving through the walls of a pot to make lamps, bulb pots or candle holders, a thin, sharp blade is needed. The cut edges must be smoothed over, as they can be razor-sharp after firing, as well as giving the impression that the work was left unfinished.

Bold sweeping designs can be made by drawing on soft clay with the back of a fingernail or the handle of a spoon (see illustration 47).

46. Judy Cunningham-Smith, lidded earthenware slab jars. Etched design filled with dark blue transparent glaze, 21cm and 14cm

47. Judy Cunningham-Smith, carbonised sculpting-marl umbrella stand with thumbnail decoration, 42cm

Texturing

Pots with roughened surfaces, generally referred to as 'textured', can be very attractive.

There are several methods of producing textures. Grog, sand or clay shavings can be sprinkled over wet clay or on to a design painted with wet slip. Alternatively, the clay can be roughened with any implement which will produce the desired effect; objects used in this way in our studio have included hacksaw and Surform blades, rough stones, broken shells, table forks and a food grater. The final effect is governed also by the composition and consistency of the body.

Interesting patterns can be produced by using different grades and colours of grog combined with burnishing or carving to highlight the patterns.

If the clay is to be rolled out to make slabs for building, a variety of surfaces can be obtained by rolling out on cloth, sacking, netting, textured wallpaper, grog or sand. Care should be taken to preserve the markings when making the joins; if it is too difficult to keep the original pattern, then either the joins may be deliberately smoothed, so that the texturing forms a panel on each slab, or a contrasting texture may be applied after the joins are made.

Appliqué

This is decoration in the form of pieces of clay stuck on to the completed work. Coils, balls, flowers, leaves and geometrical shapes are a few suggestions. The pot and the decoration must have the same moisture content, but different bodies can be used as long as the shrinkage is the same. By mixing powdered oxides into the clay, decorations of differing colours can be produced.

48. Carol Jones, lidded earthenware jar built up using lumps. Appliqué design, 36cm

If the clay is wet and sticky the decoration can be rolled or pressed on to the pot. If it is not sticky, then both surfaces must be roughened and thickish slip applied before they are joined.

Another version of appliqué is 'sprigging'. A design is carved in reverse into a block of plaster of Paris, or leather-hard clay which must then be fired to a soft biscuit to provide an absorbent mould. Clay of the same moisture content as the pot to be decorated is pressed into the mould and levelled off by wiping with a wet sponge, making the surface flat and sticky. The mould is then pressed against the pot with a rolling action which causes the clay sprig to stick to the pot and pull out of the mould. New plaster moulds must be cleaned so that no loose plaster is left in them to contaminate the sprigs. This is best done by filling the mould repeatedly with pieces of scrap clay until the clay comes away clean. This clay must then be discarded, as the plaster in it would cause it to shatter if fired. Clay moulds will last much longer than plaster because they are not affected by repeated wetting and drying.

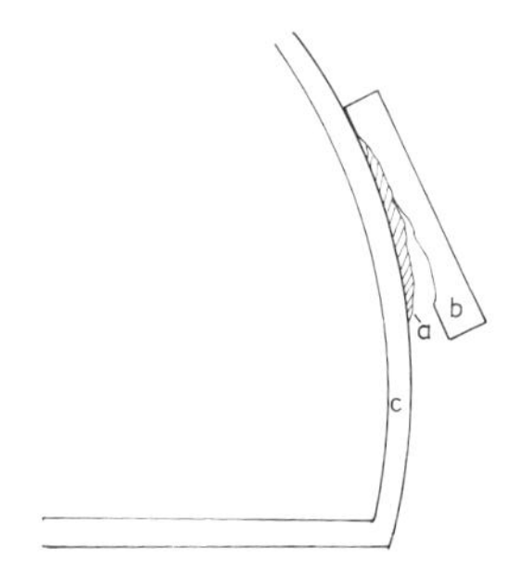

49. Application of a sprig: *a* sprig; *b* plaster block; *c* wall of pot

Slip and Sgraffito

The American Indians of New Mexico and Arizona are experts at this type of decoration. They have a tradition of making simple hand-built pots and decorating them with very intricate and beautiful designs using slip. These pots are generally fired in a simple open fire fuelled with dried dung.

We encourage students to use this method of decoration on pots which are to be fired in the bush fire or updraft kiln. The slip must have the same shrinkage as the body from which the pot is made. Brown and white earthenware bodies supplied by the same firm generally have the same shrinkage, but slips of contrasting colours are usually produced by the addition of powdered oxides to one body.

The preparation of slip is much the same as the process of reconstituting clay. Powder some dried body by hammering or using a grater, add the powder to water—not water to powder—and stir until thoroughly mixed. Pass the resulting slurry through an 80 mesh sieve and leave it to settle out overnight. Siphon off the spare water and stir the slip very carefully, making sure that no air bubbles are introduced into it. Any vigorous stirring will cause bubbles to form, and these will spoil the application of the slip to the pot—when they burst, as the slip dries out, a crater is left on the surface which cannot be filled without leaving an even more noticeable mark. The consistency of the slip should be that of double or pouring cream. If oxides are used to colour the slip, they should be added to the dry powder or to the slurry before it is sieved.

Before applying the slip to a pot, it is essential to have everything clean and all the tools ready to hand: a clean sponge, a dish of clean water, a wire tray, a ladle and a jug. When covering a pot completely with slip rather than just painting a design, it is essential to work quickly and without hesitation in order to avoid wetting the pot too much or getting marks in the slip covering due to uneven thickness. If the pot gets too wet it will collapse. The best stage at which to apply a coating of slip is when the pot is leather-hard. It is advisable to practise all the movements of application before actually using the slip.

With a flat article, such as a plate or dish, rest it on one hand and pour in a ladle full of slip, put the ladle down and use both hands to turn and tip the pot so that the slip runs over the rim all the way round and back into the bucket. By the time the whole of the rim is covered, all the spare slip should have been poured out. Give the pot a slight shake or tap the hand holding it to even out the slip, sponge off any which has run down on to the outside, and place the pot on a tray. Do not touch it again until the slip has set. Any attempts to touch up mistakes or fill in gaps will only spoil the surface and make matters worse. It is far better to incorporate them into a pattern. Articles which are not flat or shallow can be dipped or the slip can be poured over them, as in glazing.

When the slip has dried to leather-hard, the pot can be burnished and a design painted over the base colour using slips of different colours, or powdered oxides suspended in water, or a combination of both. The design can be burnished or left to provide a contrast in texture as well as colour.

Simple designs painted on to the body of the pot without first applying a base coat are quite effective, but the surface of the pot will not have the perfect smoothness created by the application of the liquid slip. An alternative to painting the designs with a brush is to use a slip trailer, which works in much the same way as an icing bag (see illustration 109), but this technique needs a great deal of practice before the precision of brushwork is equalled. The ideal way to practise is to work on a clean glazed tile which can be sponged off without wasting the slip.

A marbled effect can be obtained in shallow pots by using several different colours. The separate slips should be spooned into the pot and then, by careful tipping and revolving, the colours can be mixed together to form the streaking and whorls resembling marble. Dripping a sècondary colour on to a

50. *Left*: Mollie Herbert, once-fired pinched pot with a sgraffito design cut through a slip glaze. *Right*: Connie Dixon, coiled earthenware with a sgraffito design cut through white slip, 11.5cm

base coat before it is dry and shaking the pot can produce a similar effect.

Sgraffito is an absorbing form of decoration which can produce pleasing individual results. When the slip is leather-hard, a pattern is cut or scratched through it to expose the contrasting clay below. A metal meat skewer or a small sharp twist drill is the ideal tool for this purpose, as the clay swarf tends to be channelled away from the cut, leaving it clean. The cutting tool must be kept absolutely clean to avoid smudging and contamination of the contrasting colours. Fine dental tools are also useful, and a Scarsten scraper is ideal for cleaning off large areas.

The design may take the form of a fine line drawing, or the slip may be removed over large areas to form a bolder pattern. Sgraffito work is best finished with a transparent glaze, though if the slip has been burnished it can be left unglazed and a wax polish applied.

There are two other methods of producing the effect of sgraffito. The first is to paint the pattern on to the leather-hard clay using melted paraffin wax, and then to dip or pour the slip over the pot. The wax will burn away during firing, leaving the pattern showing. The second way is to make a paper pattern, dampen it slightly with a sponge and smooth it on to the pot before applying the slip. The paper can be removed when the slip has set or, to avoid chipping the edges of the design, it can be left in place to burn off during the biscuit firing. It is not a good idea to leave the paper to burn off in any quantity or as a regular practice if using an electric kiln, as this will damage the elements. Leaves can also be used in this manner, a sprig of cypress being particularly effective.

An inlay effect can be produced by first making an incised decoration and then applying enough slip of a contrasting colour to fill in the cuts. When this has dried to leather-hard, the excess can be scraped away carefully, leaving the pattern showing.

Painting with Oxides

If, owing to lack of space and finance, one is restricted to using only two or three glazes, it is possible to obtain a wide range of effects by the use of the cheaper oxides, ie manganese and the iron oxides. These are painted on to the raw clay before firing and a clear transparent glaze or wax polish used to provide a good finish. A great variety of results can be obtained in this manner.

The oxides should be mixed in small pots with screw lids, using enough water to make the mixture easy to apply with a brush. As the oxides are only suspended in water and not dissolved, it is essential to stir the mixture every time the brush is dipped into it, making sure that all the sediment at the bottom of the pot is mixed into the water. Using a clean brush, stir the mixture, shake off any excess water and apply the oxide to the pot with a single stroke. Oxides and glazes cannot be spread on the surface of a pot in the same way as paint is spread on a wall; the single laying-on stroke is sufficient, and any further attempts at spreading will spoil the surface of the pot and mix the clay into the oxide. If more than one colour is to be used, it is a good idea to use a separate brush for each oxide mixture; in this way there is no danger of contamination, and wastage through frequent washing of the brush can be avoided. An initial rinse of the brush in the 'scrapings' jar before washing it will save what oxide remains in the bristles.

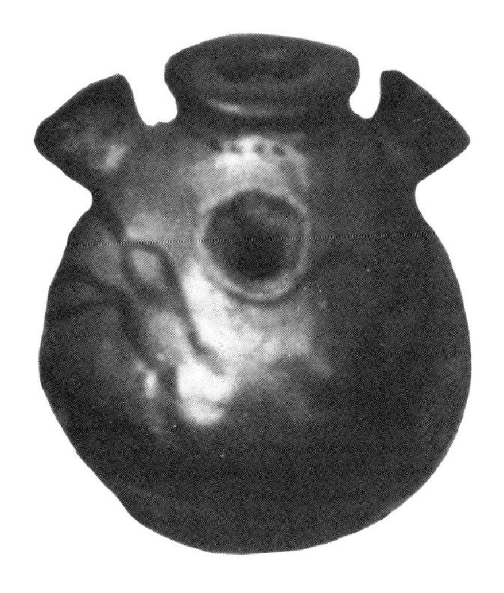

51. Edna North, bush-fired brick-clay 'promise pot' painted with iron oxides, 12cm. Some African tribes use a promise pot as one would use a written contract. A pot is made with as many orifices as there are people undertaking the agreement. Each person then whispers his part of the promise into the pot, which thus becomes the symbol of the contract. If the contract is broken or is no longer needed, the pot is broken

Suggestions for using a combination of colours are:

1. applying a base colour of iron oxide and, when this is dry, painting an intricate design of manganese oxide over it;
2. painting maganese on to the green (dry unfired) body and copper oxide over the raw transparent glaze for the second firing;
3. painting manganese and rutile on to raw clay.

It is advisable to experiment on small unimportant pots in order to get used to the strengths of the various oxides before working on larger, more precious creations.

5 Bush Firing

After a number of experiments resulting in a lot of broken pots we have worked out the following method of bush firing which we find very successful. We prefer to use the term 'bush fire', rather than 'bonfire' or 'open kiln', for the method of firing pots in the open air, because we think it is more in keeping with the traditions connected with this type of pottery work. The process, which involves direct contact between pots and fire, is suitable only for firing unglazed pottery.

Bodies suitable for this type of pottery are those with a low shrinkage, the ideal being 3 per cent or less. It is very interesting and rewarding to experiment with local clays to produce such a mixture. Preparation of such bodies is explained in Chapter 1. We have tested many bodies from a number of suppliers, using various fillers. The following we found to be suitable for bush firing:

1. Fulham Pottery sculpting marl
2. Podmore's raku body
3. Acme Marls sculpturing clay
4. A 50/50 mixture of Fulham Pottery sculpting marl and our local brick marl
5. Harrison Mayer red body with 30 per cent sifted granite dust, which must

52. Marion Hicks, bush-fired sculpting-marl slab pot with impressed decoration and burnished with iron oxides, 32cm

be properly mixed into the body. If it is not perfectly distributed the mica crystals in the dust form layers within the clay, causing the pot to disintegrate in large flakes when it is fired. The best way to ensure that it is properly distributed is to make the body into a slurry and stir the dust in. This takes less energy than kneading the dust into the plastic body. Kneading takes a long time and tends to encourage the layering of the crystals.

Because the clays vary so greatly even within relatively small areas, it is not possible to give definite instructions for bodies for bush firing. Some people will be lucky enough to have a local clay which can be fired in this way without the addition of a filler of any sort. Others will have to purchase from suppliers or experiment with local river clays to find a suitable body.

It is most important that the pots be completely dry and warm before they are subjected to the heat of the fire. The simple and economic way to do this is to dry the pots in the sun and then burn dry grass inside them to warm them prior to firing and to drive off the last of the moisture. However, we dry our work on the top of the electric kiln during a glost firing, and in very damp weather we have even put them inside the kiln and pre-heated them very slowly to 200 °C. As the firing site is across the creek from the studio, the pots are wrapped in rags or sacking to keep them warm and dry while they are being carried there.

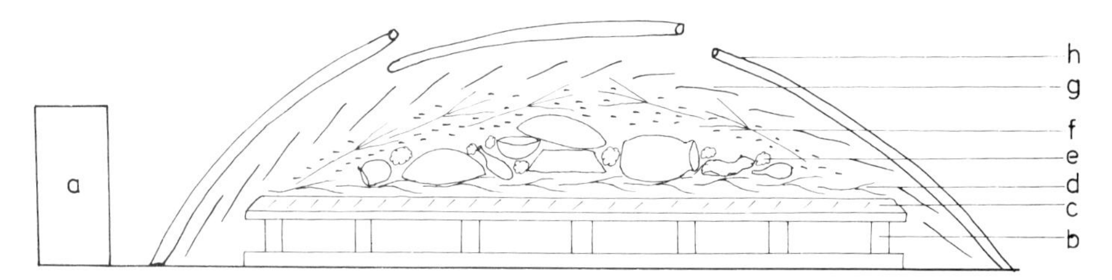

53. Cross-section of a bush fire: *a* brick or turf retaining wall; *b* cargo pallet or lattice of branches; *c* shavings, hedge trimmings or dried seaweed; *d* dry brushwood or other quick-burning material; *e* screws of dry grass or paper between the pots to be fired; *f* shavings or dry grass and brushwood; *g* green hedge trimmings if necessary, to hold back the flames for warming; *h* branches or timber

The fire is built inside a circle of bricks three or four layers high with gaps between them to allow air to pass through. This is only to contain the fire, and a circle of turf or earth would do just as well. Stones should not be used, as there is a very real danger of their exploding as the fire grows hot. We use a scrap cargo pallet from the nearby docks for a base, but a latticework of branches or timber would do just as well. The base should not be packed too tightly, as its purpose is to provide access for air so that the flames can heat the underside of the pots before the structure collapses. This base is covered with a thin layer of coarse shavings, hedge trimmings, dry seaweed or any fine material which will smoulder before flaming, followed by dry brushwood or any other quick-burning material.

54. Laying the base for a bush fire

55. Pots placed on the base ready to cover

56. Holding back the fire while the pots warm through

The pots are stacked carefully on their bases, on their sides or upside down—whichever is the most stable position—so that they will not roll on to one another as the wood burns away. Heavy solid structures should be in the middle at the bottom where they can do no damage to the more delicate pieces and will also receive the greatest heat. Screws of newspaper or dry grass are stuffed gently between the pots and into the edge of the base layer. A layer of dry material such as wood shavings and brushwood covers the pots, followed by green hedge trimmings or other slow-burning material.

The fire is lit at the base on all sides, and prevented from blazing until the pots have been heated through by the smoke. This is done by damping down any flames with green grass, seaweed, leaves or other similar material for about half an hour. In warmer, dryer climates than ours this is not so necessary, and if the pots have been heated to 200°C beforehand it is not necessary to hold the fire back at all. In fact, a hotter firing is achieved from a loose fire which is not clogged by too much ash from the damping fuel. Once well alight, the fire is kept stoked with branches or timber (placed on and against the pile rather than balanced across it) for about an hour or until the pots show red-hot. The fire is then covered with corrugated iron, to spread the heat out to the edges of the pile, and left to burn down. This step of covering the fire is not essential and can be omitted if corrugated iron is not available. The pots on the outside of the pile will then be slightly lower-fired than those in the centre, but this can be remedied to some extent by making the base of the fire a good 80cm greater in diameter than the pile of pots, so that in effect all the pots are in the middle of the fire.

We found that pots left in the fire until they were cool enough to handle very often broke. This was because the part in contact with the ashes stayed hot while the rest was cooled very rapidly by the air. So we now remove them while they are still very hot, using long tongs or a stout wooden stick, and plunge them into a bath of hot tan liquor, prepared previously by boiling oak bark in water. This seems to fix any oxide decoration and enhance the natural colours of the pot.

If a pot has a small opening it must be lowered very carefully into the bath without immersing the hole. If the liquor is allowed to enter the pot it will immediately turn to steam which cannot escape quickly enough through the hole and so the pot generally bursts under the strain. There is also a danger that steam which does manage to escape through the hole will cause severe burns to the person holding the pot.

57. The bush fire well alight, with the tannin solution heating on the wall

58. Hot fired pots being dipped into the tan liquor

59. Rolling a large pot out of the fire. The pot, coiled in sculpting marl by Grace Upton, was carried to the firing site on the sheet, which was then 'sacrificed' to avoid damaging the pot in trying to rescue it. As the pot was built next to the electric kiln, it did not need to undergo a special drying process before firing

If an article is too large to handle with the tongs, a path is cleared through the wall of bricks and the pot is rolled out of the fire and kept rolling while the tan liquor is either poured over it or slapped on with a cloth. It is better to use the cloth, because pouring is very wasteful and the resulting hot puddle under the pot can be a great inconvenience. It must be impressed upon spectators that the bricks, which may be very hot, should not be touched.

Undecorated pots can be carbonised by removing them from the fire while they are still very hot and burying them in a pile of fine sawdust, dry leaves or dry grass. After ten minutes they should be removed and plunged into the tan liquor. This process produces a good black finish which can be almost metallic in appearance if the pot is highly burnished.

All pots which are not to be used to contain food or water should be waxed or oiled while they are still hot with any type of household polish, beeswax, shoe polish or teak oil, then polished when cold.

This typc of firing can be done whatever the weather and at any time of the year. We have built a fire in the rain, with people holding corrugated iron over the pots until they were covered with fuel and the fire was well alight; when we removed the pots from the fire the rain did not cause them any damage.

In strong wind some protection will be needed to windward of the fire, otherwise the pots on that side will not be fired high enough. This can be effected by building the wall higher and omitting any air holes, or by using corrugated iron or something similar as a windbreak.

60. Pots ready for bush firing

A single large pot can be fired as follows. The pot is pre-heated by standing it upside down on three bricks over a small smouldering fire until it is warmed right through. The fire can then be built up around it by leaning sticks and timber up against it. The timbers can be quite thick, and it does

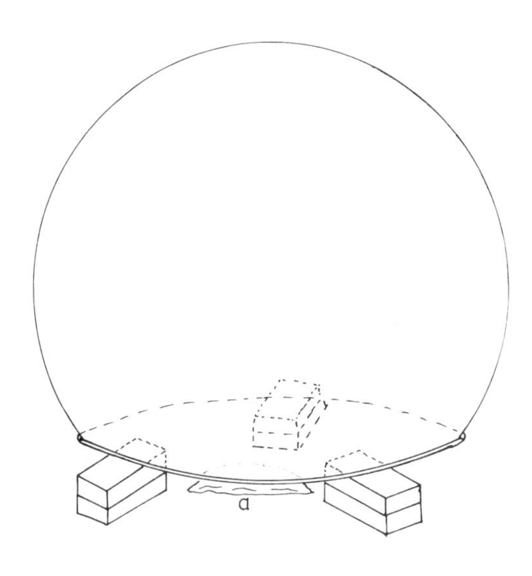

61. Warming a large pot through before firing: *a* small fire

not matter if the pot is not completely covered all round as this allows a good flow of air to the fire, which should be kept stoked by placing more timber on end against it until the pot shows signs of getting red-hot. The fire is then allowed to die down and the pot rolled out and treated in the same way as the smaller ones.

Successful firings of pots made for bush firing can be carried out in an open grate indoors. However, in this case very great care must be taken, and firing of solid sculptures should not be attempted as these are more likely to explode.

The pots must be completely dry before they are put into the fire. They can be dried by very slow heating in a domestic cooking stove to just over 200°C, which is the critical point. This reduces the danger of explosions, which we found to our cost tended to shoot into the room not only pieces of hot clay but half the fire as well, despite the fact that a good small-mesh guard was in use.

Make sure that there is a safe place to stand the pot when it is removed from the fire, and if tan liquor is used remember that it will stain quite badly if spilt on carpets or wooden floors.

6 Sawdust Firing

This is a very simple way of firing pottery which can be done in the garden or yard. It results in an attractive black finish, though the ware, which is low-fired to about 600°C, will be very brittle and definitely not waterproof. It is, however, a good way to introduce children to the techniques and responsibilities connected with the firing of pottery.

Pots for firing in sawdust should be made from a low-firing earthenware body or a brick clay which can be dug locally. It is an added interest for children if the clay they use is dug and prepared by themselves. The techniques for preparing such a clay are described in Chapter 1. The clay must have some sort of filler added, such as fine silica sand or grog. The sand can be purchased from a garden shop if only small quantities are needed. This filler reduces the contraction and expansion of the clay and makes the body semi-porous so that moisture can escape during the firing without shattering the pot.

Solid models can be fired in sawdust as long as they are well dried before firing and there is plenty of filler in the body, which must be thoroughly wedged so that no air pockets are present within it. The strength of the pot can be greatly increased by burnishing before firing (see Chapter 4).

The sawdust can be from any type of wood, but the resin from pine sometimes produces beautiful blue and silver markings on the pots. The 'kiln' can be made from ordinary house bricks, turf or an old dustbin with

62. Sawdust-fired pots polished with sour milk. *Left and right*: Mollie Herbert, pinched. *Centre*: John Herbert, coiled, 13.5cm

holes punched in the sides for ventilation. Apart from the actual kiln and sawdust, the items needed are: kindling and paper to light a small starter fire on top of the packed sawdust; a metal lid such as a dustbin lid or a piece of corrugated iron to cover the kiln once the fire is alight; and a little sour milk or wax polish to polish the pots after firing.

We use bricks to make our kiln, varying the size to suit the number of pots to be fired. At least 15cm should be allowed between the pots and the side of the kiln, otherwise they will not be heated properly. The first two courses of bricks should be laid with air spaces between them. If turf or a dustbin is used, holes should be made in the first 15cm. This bottom section is best filled with coarse sawdust or shavings, as otherwise the fine dust tends to compact so that it does not burn properly and air is prevented from flowing to the rest of the kiln.

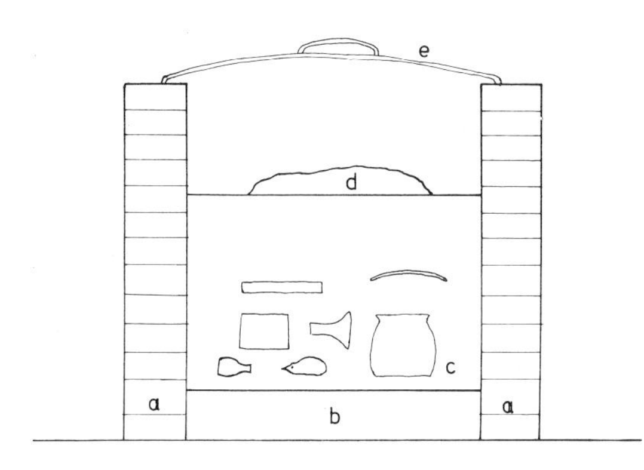

63. Section showing the loading of a sawdust kiln: *a* containing wall (or dustbin); *b* coarse shavings; *c* pots loaded in layers of sawdust; *d* small fire to start the sawdust burning; *e* dustbin lid or other metal cover

Build up the bricks or turf to the required height without leaving any more air holes, and then place the pots so that they will not roll when the sawdust burns away. If more than one layer of pots is to be fired, the heaviest should be in the bottom layer, lying on their sides or upside down. Pots should not be filled with sawdust; it will not burn because of the lack of air within the pot, and heat will be used up in warming the cold sawdust, resulting in a lower firing temperature. Cover the first layer of pots with 6cm of sawdust and place the next heaviest pots carefully so that when the sawdust is burnt they will rest between the pots below, reducing the risk of rolling and breakage. More layers can be added in this way, but if too many pots are fired at once those at the bottom of the pile after firing are likely to be broken. Generally, three layers are enough. It is better to do two firings or to widen the circle, if this is possible, than to make the kiln higher.

The top layer of pots should be covered with 15cm of sawdust, on which a fire is lit using the kindling and paper. Once the fire is well alight the 'lid' must be put into position. This fire ignites the sawdust, which should smoulder, not flame. If it does burst into flames once the fire has burnt out, it should be damped down with more sawdust and the draught cut down, either by placing a sheet of corrugated iron to windward of the kiln or by plugging some of the holes with mud.

Once the sawdust is smouldering well it can be left to burn unattended. The length of time required for it to burn through completely will vary with the wind strength and the quantity of sawdust in the kiln, but it is usually between eight and twenty-four hours. We find it safer to remove the pots from the kiln while they are still quite warm if this is possible. As in bush firing, if they are left to cool in the kiln the parts in contact with the hot ash remain hot while the exposed areas cool rapidly, creating stresses in the clay and causing the pots to crack.

Sour milk rubbed into the pots while they are still warm gives a very good finish to the burnished surface. However, if you cannot face the idea of using this traditional finishing agent, beeswax or ordinary furniture polish can be used instead.

7 The Updraft Kiln

A simple updraft kiln provides an interesting way of firing pottery if a plentiful supply of wood can be obtained for fuel. A site well away from buildings and trees is essential. The site need not be level; it is a saving in bricks and labour if the kiln can be built into a bank, as the firing chamber is best located slightly above the firebox.

Owing to the variations in the kiln atmosphere, caused by burning wood and flame flashes, reduction and ash deposits can occur on the pottery, making the colour and finish of the ware very unpredictable. The unloading of the kiln can be a very exciting adventure especially if the wood burnt had paint on it or contained a lot of resin.

The kiln works on the very simple principle of a firebox leading to a firing chamber with a restricted entrance and supported shelves which are on a level with the top of the firebox. The firing chamber has a conical top leading into a fairly high chimney to draw the fire.

We obtained permission from the Devon County Council to build such a kiln on the public open space only two hundred metres across the creek from our studio. This area was originally a rubbish dump which was levelled and grassed over about twenty years ago. The first kiln we made was built entirely from old bricks and scrap iron washed out of the edges of the dump by the sea and plastered together with mud collected from the centre of the creek.

64. Red earthenware with grog filler fired in the updraft kiln Mk 1. *Left*: Brian Adams, vase, 20cm. *Centre*: Pat Adams, burnished plaque. *Right*: Lydia Cunningham, solid figure

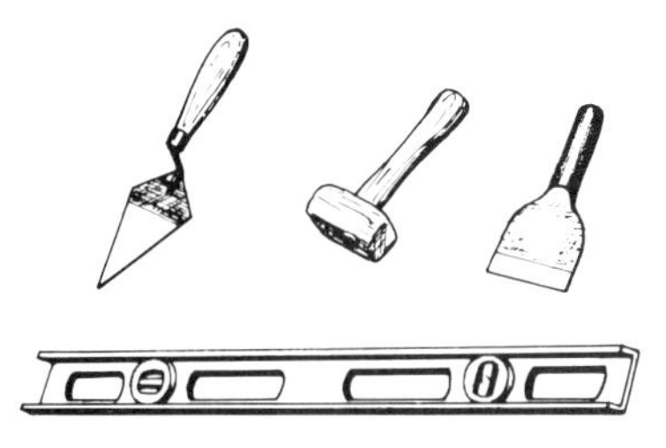

65. Tools needed for building the updraft kiln

This kiln has just been replaced by a more permanent one—still using the bricks from the dump, but with a mortar mixture of two parts of sand from the beach to one part of powdered local brick clay. New fire bars and supports for the firebox and loading doorways were also made. The new kiln has a capacity of 0.2m³. To make a kiln of this size, the following materials are needed:

Approximately 600 standard house bricks
An assortment of half-bricks and broken odd shapes to fill in gaps on the outer surface of the circular structure
Nine 45cm lengths of 2.5cm diameter iron rod
Three 55cm lengths of 5cm × 0.5cm mild steel
50kg powdered brick clay or powdered brown earthenware
100kg fine building sand

66. Building the updraft kiln Mk 1

A pillar in the form of a cylinder 15cm in diameter, 24.75cm high, with walls 2.5cm thick, made from sculpting marl or some other strong refractory clay

Six shelves made from the same body as the pillar, with the dimensions shown in illustration 67

A block made of clay the size of a half-brick, with a tapering hole in the centre to act as a spyhole

A tapered plug to fit the spyhole

The layout of the kiln should be designed so that the firebox entrance faces into the prevailing wind. Ours is built into a small bank so that the floor of the firebox is about 15cm lower than that of the firing chamber. This means that an ash pit need not be dug and the floor of the firing chamber need not be raised.

Illustrations 67-85 give step-by-step details of the construction of this kiln.

67-85: Updraft Kiln Mk 2, designed by John Herbert

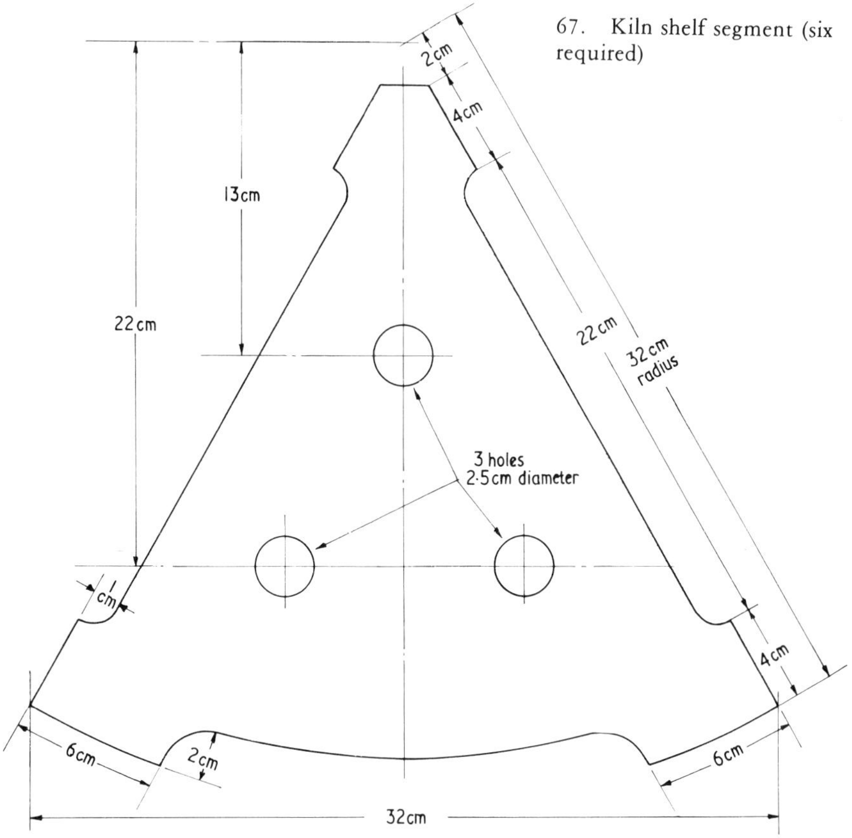

67. Kiln shelf segment (six required)

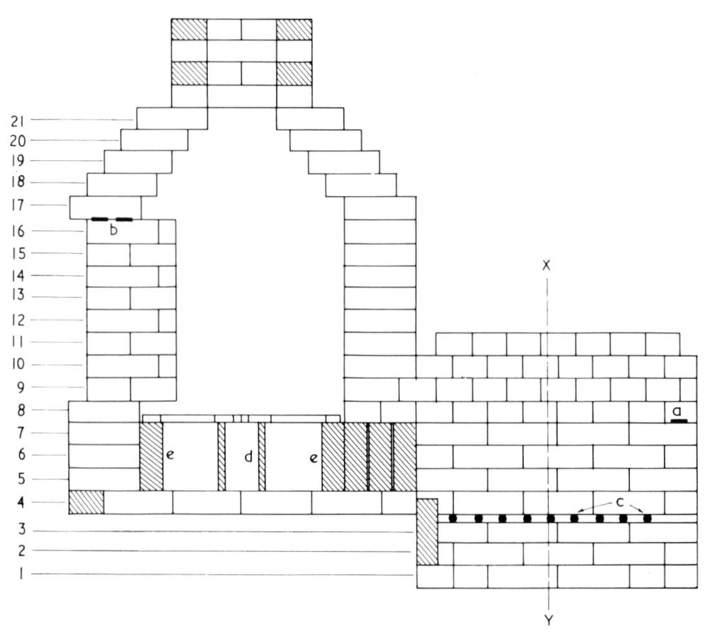

68. Section through kiln: *a, b* doorway supports, 55cm × 5cm × 0.5cm mild steel; *c* fire bars, 45cm × 2.5cm diameter iron rod; *d* central supporting pillar for shelf segments; *e* outer support bricks. XY indicates section shown in illustration 69*A*

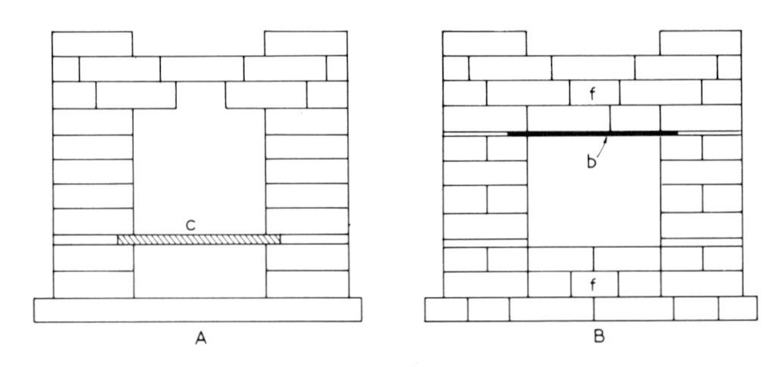

69. *A* section XY through firebox: *c* fire bar
B front view of firebox: *b* doorway support bar;
f removable damper brick

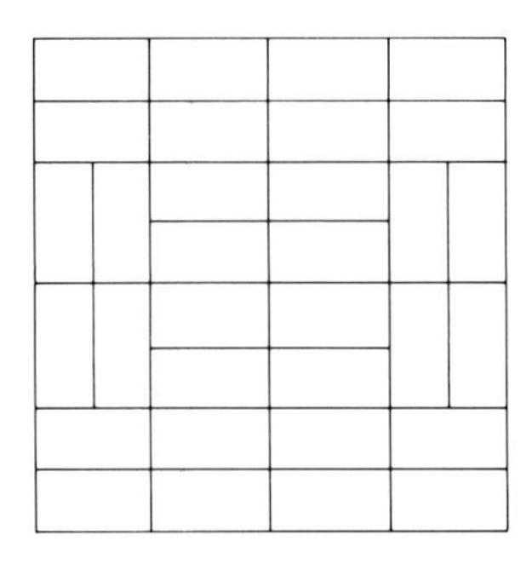

70. Course 1: firebox base

Opposite:
74. Courses 5 and 7: *x* space filled with mortar and bits of brick; *d* centre support pillar; *e* outer support bricks. Doorway support on course 7 (see illustration 69*B*)

75. Course 6: *d* support pillar; *e* support bricks

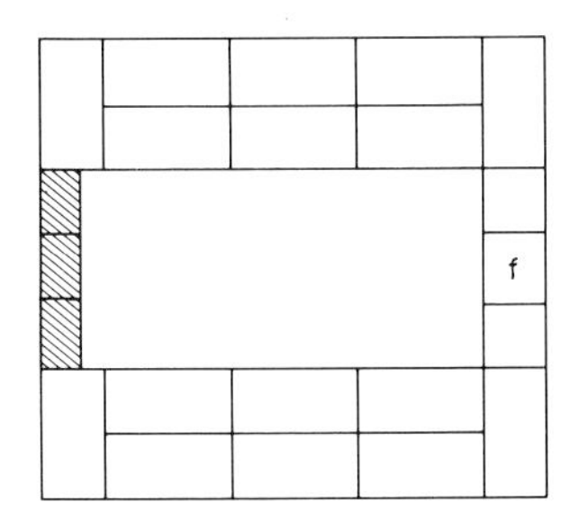

71. Course 2: *f* removable damper brick

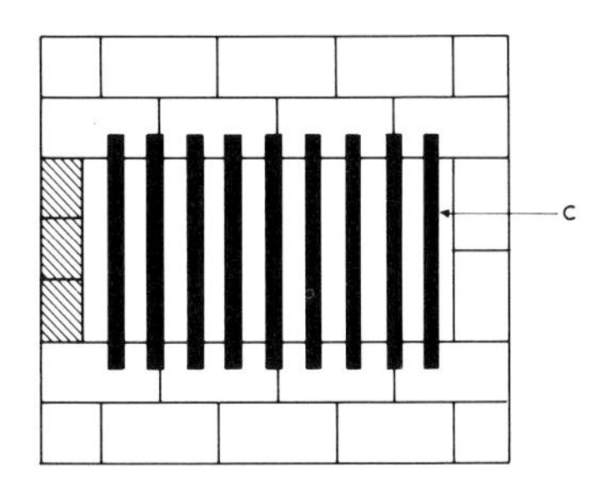

72. Course 3: *c* fire bars

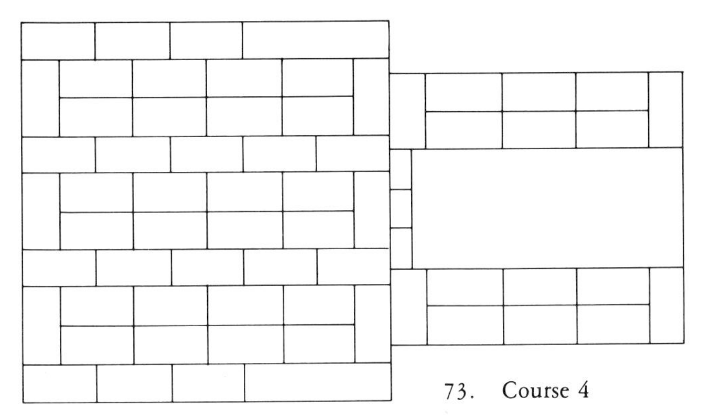

73. Course 4

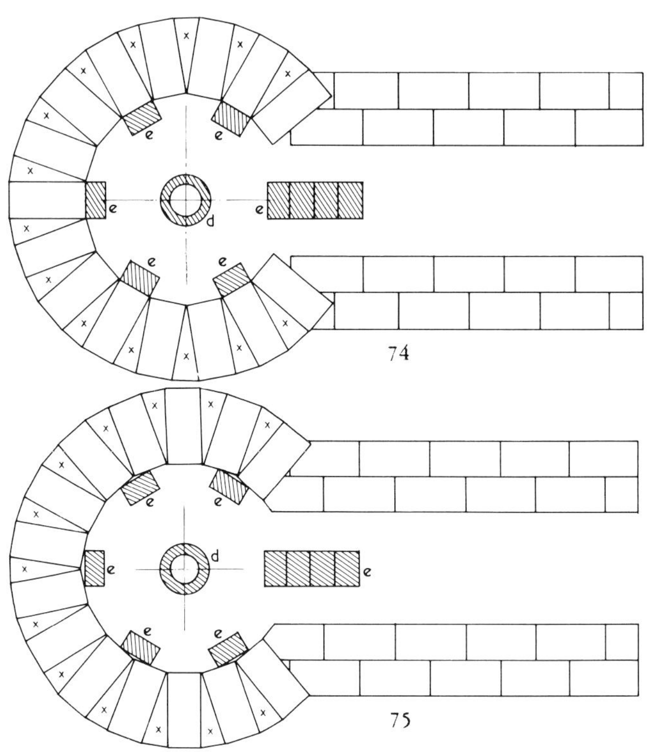

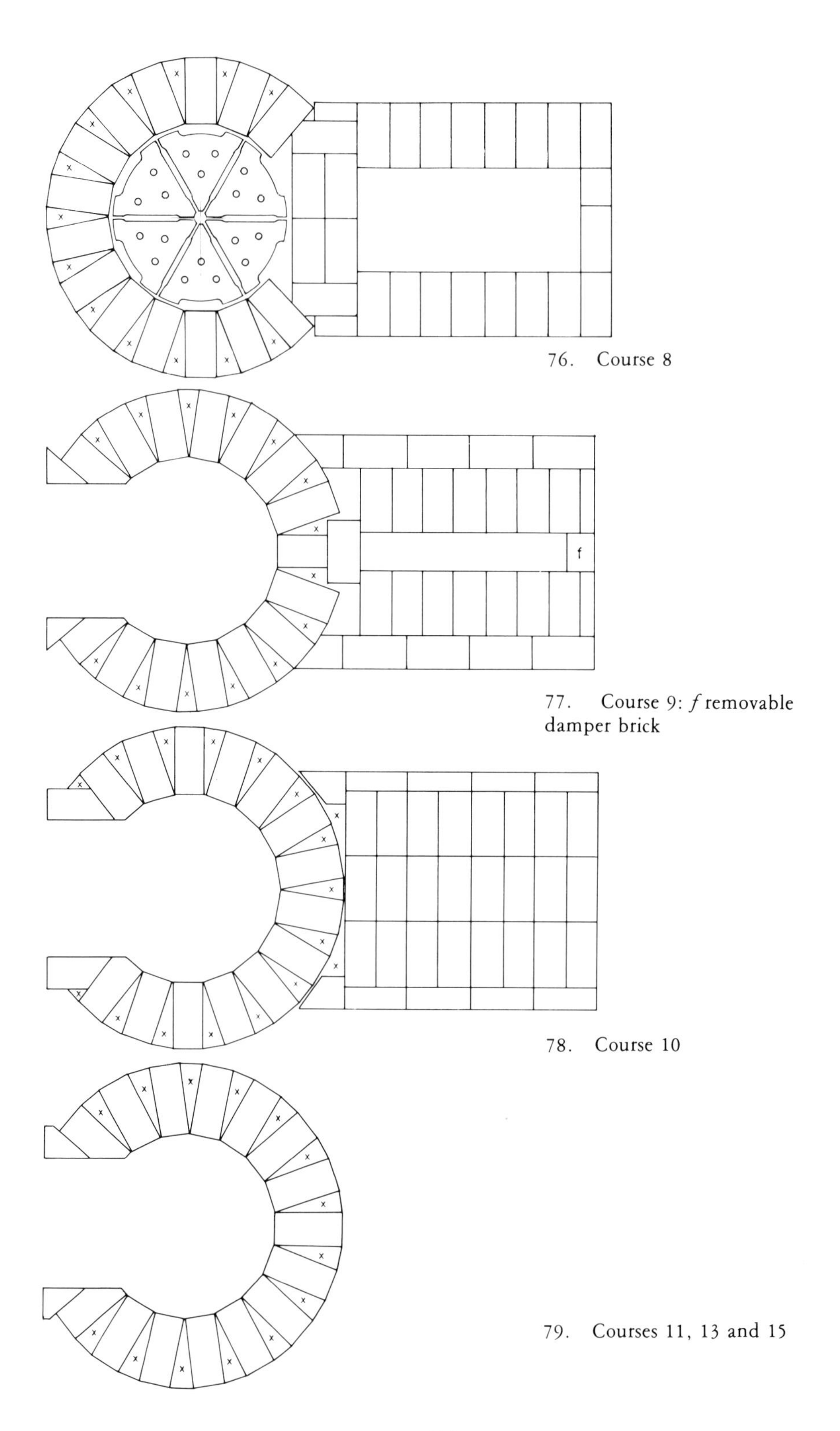

76. Course 8

77. Course 9: *f* removable damper brick

78. Course 10

79. Courses 11, 13 and 15

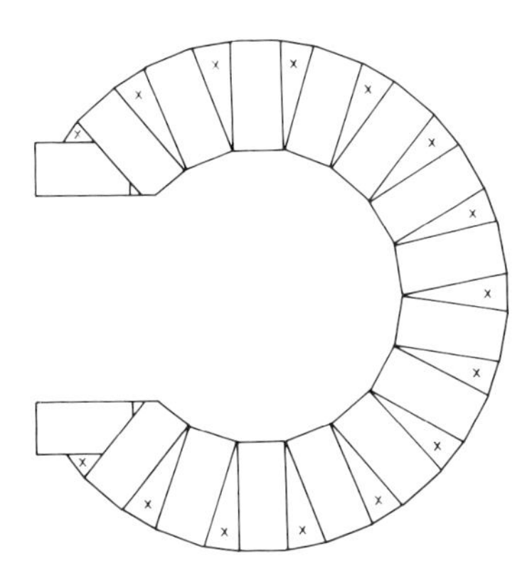

80. Courses 12, 14 and 16

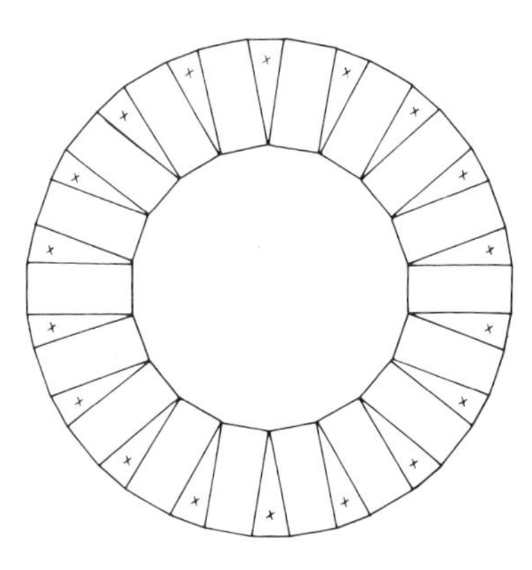

81. Course 17

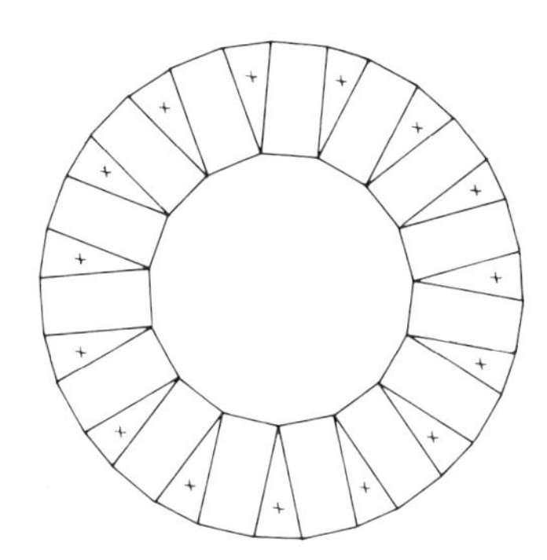

82. Course 18

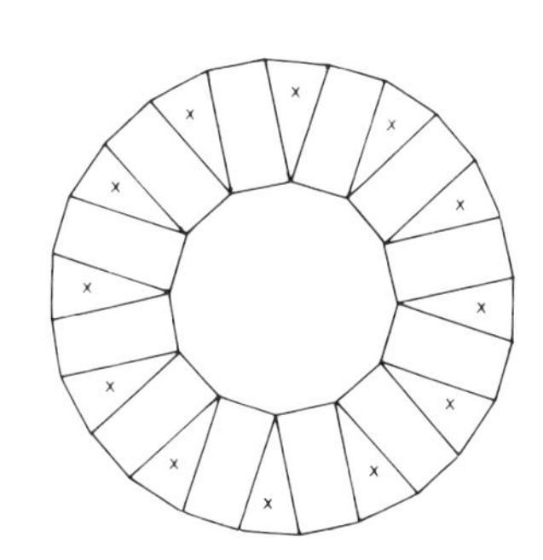

83. Course 19

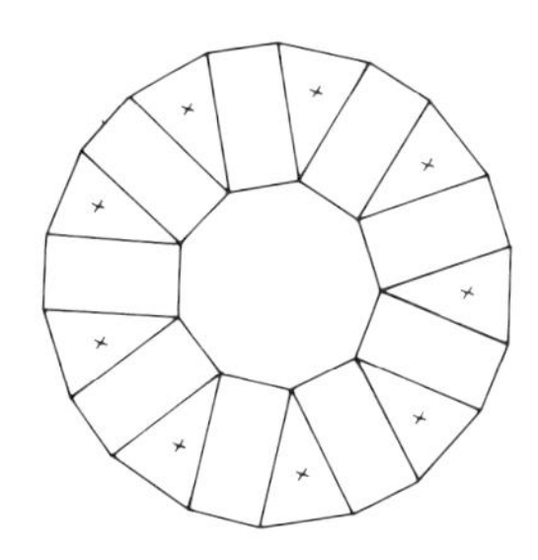

84. Course 20

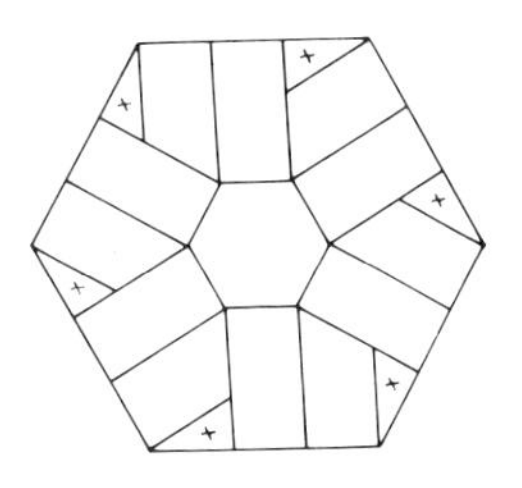

85. Course 21

When building is completed, the kiln must be dried out. The shelves, spyhole block and pillar may be fired during this process if no electric kiln is available, but otherwise the kiln should be empty. Fill in the loading doorway with loose bricks and set the spyhole block in the centre; if it is being fired in the kiln, use a piece of firebrick which can easily be removed. Plaster over the cracks between these bricks with the usual mortar mix. The kiln is dried out by lighting a small fire in the entrance of the firebox. This fire can gradually be built up until the kiln shows red-hot through the spyhole.

The entrance to the firebox will have to be restricted during firing, the extent of the restriction depending on the direction and strength of the wind. Bricks can be stacked up in the entrance and the top ones removed for stoking; we use a large firebrick from the inside of an old night storage heater with a row of bricks on top to allow for stoking. Ventilation beneath the fire bars can be controlled by a damper in the form of a loose brick which can be turned to close or open the hole. If the fire burns too quickly the bottom damper can be closed and the top stoking bricks removed to allow a cooling draught to enter across the top of the fire. This will be heated by the time it reaches the firing chamber and will not harm the pots, but it will stop the fire drawing up. Fairly good control of the fire can be obtained with practice. It is wise to use asbestos gloves when handling the bricks during stoking, and to stand them with the cool end uppermost so that one cannot accidentally pick them up by the hot end.

As soon as the fire is lit, any gaps in the walls will be indicated by smoke leaking out. These must be filled with mortar as they appear, and a watch should be kept throughout the firing so that as the mortar shrinks between the bricks the gaps can be filled. We have found that the most economical and successful method of filling the cracks is to throw dollops of wet mortar at them rather than try to use a trowel. The force of the throw causes the mortar to spread into any irregularities and to stick.

Pots for firing in an updraft kiln should be made from a body with a filler of grog or sand to enable it to withstand the thermal shock of the firing. Granite dust can be used as long as the pots are not worked too much and are not too highly burnished. If the body is well worked, the mica crystals in the granite dust tend to lie parallel with the surface of the pot, and during the firing this causes the pot to disintegrate in flakes. The same thing happens if the dust is not mixed into the clay properly. We have found that Fulham Pottery sculpting marl, Podmore's raku mixture and Acme Marls sculpturing clay generally have 100 per cent success rates in firing. They give a creamy buff colour with reduced areas on the fired ware. Both Fulham Pottery and Harrison Mayer's brown earthenware bodies with one-third by volume of fine silica sand or grog also give excellent results, especially when highly burnished. Pots with a coating of slip and painted oxide decoration are very attractive but must be well burnished, especially in the case of the oxides.

Loading the Updraft Kiln

Pots can be stacked one on top of another and inside other pots, as in a normal biscuit firing. It is wise to place weighty, heavily grogged pots on the

86. Pots loaded ready for firing in the updraft kiln Mk 1

shelf just above the entrance to the firebox, and anywhere else where they will be in direct contact with the flames, as these pots will be better able to take the thermal shocks involved. Lighter pots made from finer bodies can be placed in and on top of the heavier ones.

When the kiln is as full as is practical, or when all pottery to be fired has been placed, the doorway should be bricked up very carefully, making sure that the pots are not disturbed, and not forgetting the spyhole block. Heat indicators known as 'pyrometric cones' (see p. 88) can be placed within the kiln if a record of the temperatures reached is required. However, since the presence of fly ash from the wood fire tends to lower the melting point of the cones, the indicated temperature will be rather higher than that actually achieved.

When the kiln is loaded and closed up, a small fire should be lit at the front of the firebox and kept burning for about an hour. It can then be built up gradually until it almost fills the box. Do not push wood too close to the entrance to the firing chamber, or the vents will become blocked with embers. As soon as the fire is well alight, the door can be filled in, leaving space for stoking at the top in the manner described for drying the kiln. The temperature within the firing chamber can be checked by observing through the spyhole. The progression is from black to a very dull red, followed by bright red when the temperature is between 600°C and 800°C, orange-red between 800°C and 1000°C, and yellow at 1000°C. The latter is the ideal temperature for this type of firing; above it the burnishing tends to be destroyed. This temperature can be reached in five to six hours, depending on how tightly the kiln is filled.

As soon as the required temperature is reached, place a kiln shelf on top of the chimney, with bricks to hold it in place. Fill in the firebox doorway and make sure that there are no leaks in the walls where the mortar has shrunk during the firing. The kiln should then be left to cool naturally. This should take at least twelve hours, and can take up to twenty-four, depending again on the packing. The temperature can be checked by looking through the spyhole. As the critical range for dunting (cracking due to rapid cooling) is between 600°C and 100°C, it is best to resist the temptation to keep looking through the hole and to open the kiln as soon as possible. Since the kiln is in the open air, the removal of the door bricks allows a blast of cold air to enter, and this can spoil many pots which would otherwise have been perfect. Patience is well rewarded in this instance.

Glazing may be done in an updraft kiln, using low-firing glazes which can give some amazing results due to the atmosphere and the presence of fly ash and other products from the burning of the wood. If glazing is to be attempted, very great care must be taken to ensure that mortar from the kiln walls does not fall on to the ware, and that pots are not touching one another or the walls. Extra shelves will also be needed in order to make full use of the space available. Pots to be glazed need only be fired to about 800°C in the biscuit firing.

87. Fired pots. The door pillar had to be dismantled to get the big urn in and out. The last firing in Mk 1

8 The Bottled Propane Gas Makeshift Kiln

This simple way of firing pottery is much used in schools in Australia, where facilities and finance are not always readily available and where the cost of the commercially supplied kilns—oil-, electricity- and gas-fired—is not justified. It is a method which we have tried with groups of children, with very satisfactory results. The children can be involved during the whole process, since the time needed for building and firing the kiln is so short. A normal biscuit firing using a heavily grogged clay can be completed in about four hours, the exact time depending on how tightly the kiln is packed and how sheltered it is from wind. It is also a satisfactory process for the self-sufficient potter who has not the facilities for more permanent and sophisticated kilns.

Russell Cowan Pty Ltd of Australia have produced a booklet called 'Lo-Fire', written by Barnacoat and Polglase, who have done considerable research into the use of bottled gas makeshift kilns. In it they give very detailed advice on construction, firing and glazing with specially prepared low-firing glazes.

The materials needed for building the kiln are very simple: fifty-nine standard house bricks plus one half-brick which should preferably be a firebrick. All bricks are loosely placed using no mortar. The following pages give detailed instructions for building and firing the kiln.

88. Children's work fired in the bottled gas makeshift kiln

Base Layout
24 bricks placed on level ground in the open, away from buildings and not in a hollow where escaped gas could accumulate and cause an explosion.

The bricks must be set evenly with the flat surfaces uppermost so that the side walls of the kiln are perfectly stable and the ware will not topple over on an uneven floor. A thin layer of sand spread underneath the bricks makes it easier to level them.

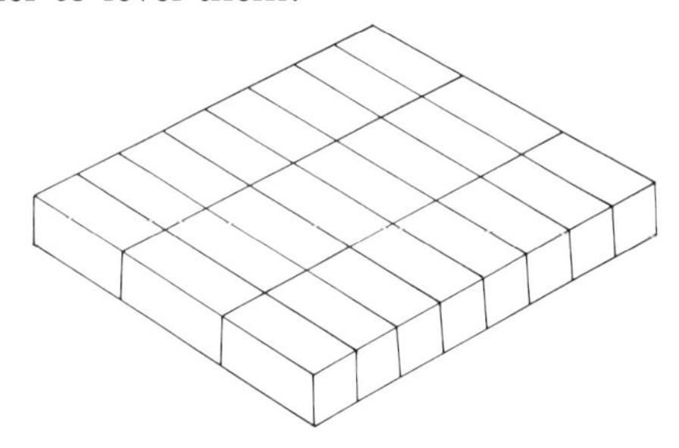

89. Gas kiln, base layer

Course 2
9½ bricks, including the half-firebrick which acts as a flame deflector in the inlet and one whole brick standing on end in front of the outlet as a roof support.

Course 3
8 bricks: 2 bridging the gap across the flame outlet vent, 2 across the inlet and 4 on the side walls.

Course 4
7 bricks: 2 across the back wall, 1 on the flame inlet and 4 on the side walls, with the 2 front ones corbelled (set in) slightly to carry the roof bricks.

Course 5
9 bricks to form the roof: 2 on the back wall, 4 set bridging the gaps between the rear side walls and the centre supporting brick, 2 set across the front corbelled bricks and 1 on the front wall.

Two spare bricks remain to be used to close the vents after firing is completed.

A clay which can withstand the thermal shock of the direct gas flame, such as sculpting marl, a raku mixture or any coarsely grogged earthenware body, should be used for pottery to be fired in this type of kiln. Solid sculptures can be fired as well as hollow pots, as long as they are well dried before firing. Remove the roof bricks in order to load the kiln. In a biscuit firing the ware can be packed tightly, but it is best to pack it more loosely at the front of the

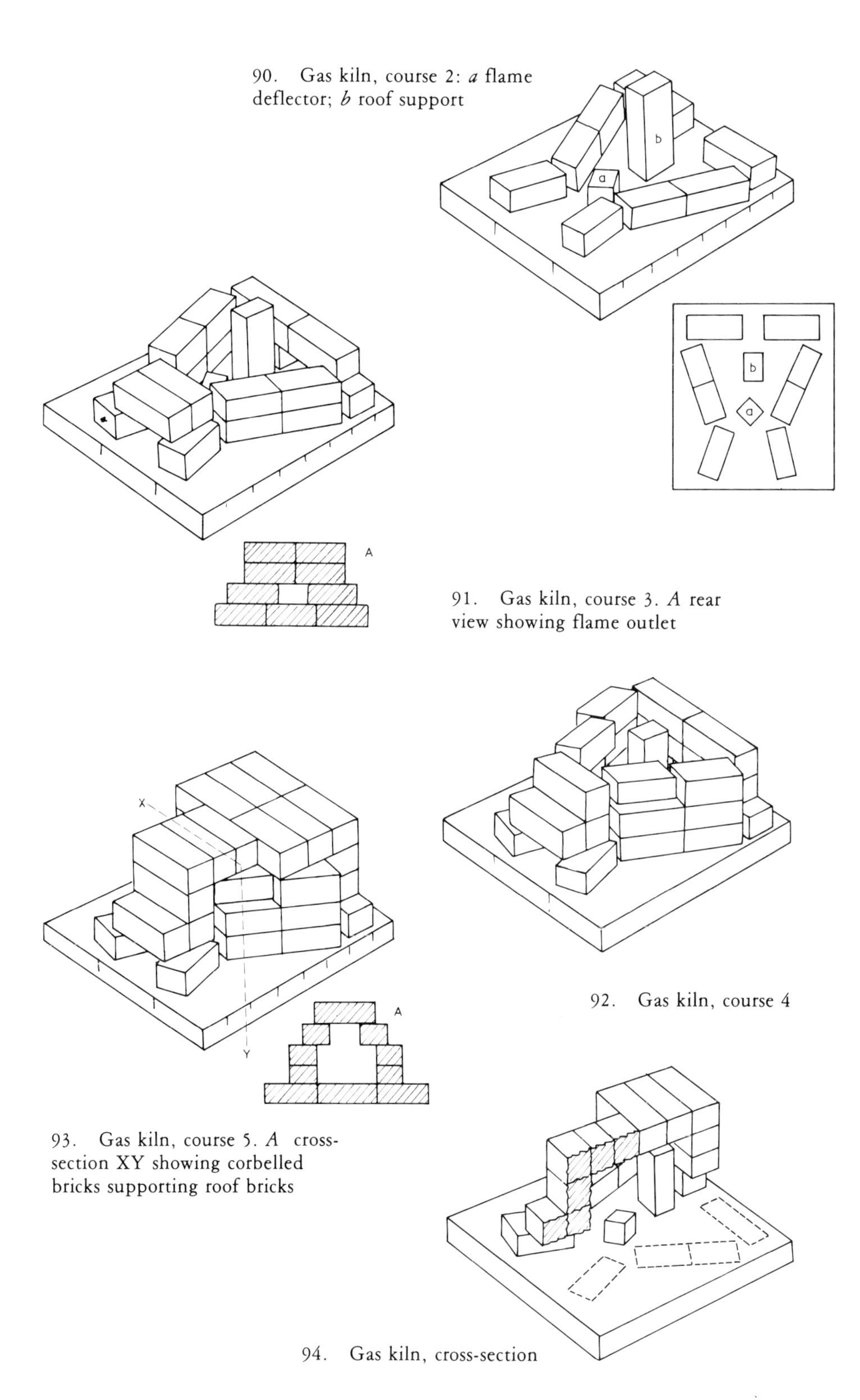

90. Gas kiln, course 2: *a* flame deflector; *b* roof support

91. Gas kiln, course 3. *A* rear view showing flame outlet

92. Gas kiln, course 4

93. Gas kiln, course 5. *A* cross-section XY showing corbelled bricks supporting roof bricks

94. Gas kiln, cross-section

kiln to ensure that the heat circulates properly through to the flame outlet. For a biscuit firing between 7 and 9kg of ware will fit into a kiln built from 57½ bricks.

A second firing can be made to glaze the ware, using the special low-firing glazes. In this case the pots must be placed very carefully so that they do not touch each other or the walls of the kiln. They should also be placed on stilts or silica sand so that they do not stick to the floor of the kiln. If glazes are not desired, the biscuit firing can be taken up to between 800°C and 1000°C; this will give the fired ware strength and plenty of natural colour through reduction. Iron oxides can be burnished into the unfired ware to increase the colouring. This temperature range is indicated by an orange-red colour seen through the cracks in the walls.

It is essential that propane gas is used; butane is not supplied at a high enough pressure. An ideal torch assembly is the Sievert burner (no 2944) with a 50cm straight-neck tube (no 3508) and a handle (no 3487) with regulating valve and economiser valve. This assembly has the advantage that the torch can be ignited easily and the flame controlled at a comfortable distance from the kiln which, towards the end of the firing, radiates a lot of heat.

The torch is connected to a 13kg bottle of propane gas by means of a 4m connecting hose (no 17295) and a regulator valve (no 3045). The long hose means that the bottle can be kept safely away from the kiln.

It is important that the following safety precautions as laid down by Sievert should be followed very carefully when using bottled gas for firing a kiln.

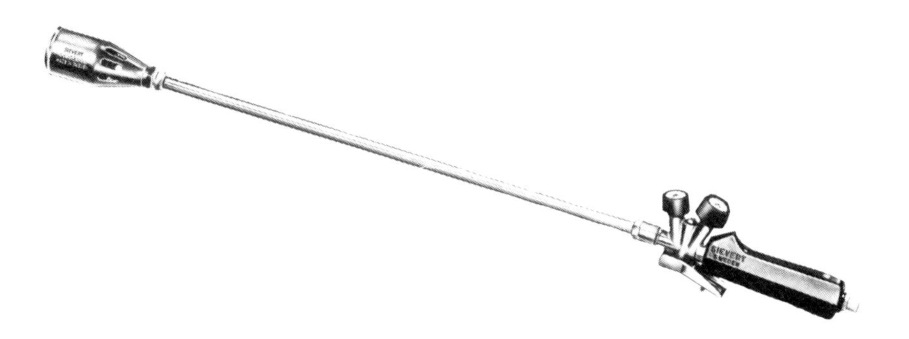

95. Sievert torch assembly for use with a makeshift gas kiln

Make sure you know how to operate your equipment correctly—seek advice from your local dealer or other experienced person.

Check your equipment regularly for leaks, especially the hose connections. Bottle Gas (LP Gas) has a distinctive smell and leaks can be detected by this smell. Never look for a leak with a naked flame but trace by smell and confirm by brushing the suspected leak with a soapy water solution.

Use only approved hoses and valves. Check hoses for kinking and wear. Wear does occur when a hose is kinked and a worn hose must be replaced with a new one—better safe than sorry. Hose clips should be checked for tightness before every firing. Appliances must be used in conjunction with an approved regulator or valve. All connections must be spanner-tightened.

Never leave an appliance unattended while it is burning. Make sure that there is no inflammable material close at hand when lighting the appliance. When you have finished with the appliance, turn off the gas at the cylinder valve so that the gas in the tube is burned off. Then close the valve of the appliance itself.

Storage cylinders must be stored in a safe place—seek the advice of your gas supplier or dealer.

Sievert appliances are carefully designed for both efficiency and safety. They will give long and trouble-free service if used correctly and well maintained. It is unwise to modify or alter the equipment without expert advice. Users are strongly urged to study the manufacturer's leaflet enclosed with each appliance.

If in doubt, seek the advice of your dealer.

When the kiln is loaded and ready to fire, turn the gas on at the cylinder, set the regulator to no 2 (28lb/in^2) and light the bypass. Place the torch on bricks so that the burner is about 2cm above the floor and pointing into the flame entrance. Depress and lock the trigger and turn on the main regulating valve to give a small flame; leave it burning for one hour.

During the next two hours gradually open the valve until it is about three-quarters open. The ware will be fired when the inside of the kiln, seen through the cracks between the bricks, shows bright cherry-red for a biscuit firing or orange-yellow for a glost firing. This temperature should be reached in about four hours, including the warming-up period.

When the correct temperature has been reached, close the cylinder valve, then the main burner and finally the pilot valve. This ensures that there is no gas left in the hose after the burner is turned off. Place a spare brick in front of the flame inlet and another across the outlet to prevent cold air being drawn through the kiln and cooling the ware too rapidly. Unload the kiln when the bricks are cool enough to handle without gloves.

9 Commercial Kilns

For a lot of the time we use a Cromartie H.T.3X.SP electric kiln with a firing chamber measuring 46cm high, 40.5cm deep and 38cm wide. It has an automatic control panel with a heat input regulator and a time switch for cut-out or control (holding) at any required temperature. When we bought this kiln in 1971 it was listed as capable of firing up to 1300°C, but as the voltage in many parts of Britain today is often below full strength, Cromartie now list the H.T.3X.SPA for stoneware temperatures. This is the same as the SP in capacity but has a 9kw rating instead of 7.5kw.

With four classes of ten students each week, our kiln seldom cools off completely during the term. It is unloaded as soon as possible after firing and another batch of pots is loaded into the warm kiln. In this way we conserve power and keep the work moving so that no one waits for more than one week for finished work to be fired.

Such a flow of work is only possible if the kiln is fitted with an automatic control. This control enables the kiln to be fired at night without loss of sleep and to make full use of special reduced rates for power supplied between 11pm and 7am. It also ensures a success rate of almost 100 per cent in firing biscuit, because the heat input regulator allows the green ware to be warmed slowly enough to expel all moisture before the critical temperature of 200°C is reached. For these reasons we think that an automatic control for the kiln is one of the essential pieces of equipment in a pottery where conservation and speed are of importance, especially in schools and communal workshops.

When choosing a kiln, the important points to consider are:

1. What fuel is to be used? As electric kilns are obtainable in quite small sizes, they are best for the hobby potter, although reduction cannot be achieved without danger to the elements. Oil-fired and gas kilns are more suitable for the commercial potter as they are supplied in too large a size for the hobby potter to run economically.
2. What power is available? Kilns with a 7.5kw rating are about the largest that can be used on a domestic supply in Britain. Larger kilns are generally designed to run on a three-phase input. In any case, the local electricity authority should always be consulted before installing any kiln with an output of more than 6kw.
3. Size of kiln? Choose one big enough to take a good-sized pot. It is better to have a kiln a little too big and to have to wait to fill it for a firing than to be restricted in the size of your creations. The cost is not all that much more for the few extra centimetres which, we have discovered, are never regretted. Our experience suggests that it is better to have the extra capacity in height rather

than width or depth, but this may not suit all potters. Before ordering the kiln, check that it will pass through the relevant doorways and up stairs when delivered. Some firms will deliver a kiln dismantled if necessary and build it on site, but it is best to check all details first.
4. Front- or top-loading kiln? Top-loading kilns are usually less expensive than front-loading, but are far less convenient: it is necessary to kneel or bend to load them, and these are not the safest positions for handling delicate work. It is easier to see what is being done as each shelf is placed in a front-loading kiln, and also easier to use half- or quarter-shelves to make full use of the space available within the kiln. Unless finance really restricts your choice it is better to pick the front-loading model.
5. Doors? If buying a front-loading kiln, decide where it will stand in the workshop and, when ordering, state whether a left-hand or right-hand opening door is required. It should open against a wall and not into the middle of the room. Kiln doors are very heavy, and the edges are sharp enough to do a great deal of harm: if something has to be picked up off the floor, it is only too easy to crack your head open on the door as you straighten up again. Also, if the kiln is being unloaded while it is still quite hot it is better to have the hot door well out of the way against a wall.
6. Safety? Under the Health and Safety at Work Act of 1974, all kilns supplied to the United Kingdom market have to be fitted with a door safety interlock device operated by a key. This key works a mechanical bolt on the kiln door, and cannot be removed until the door is securely bolted. The same key is then used to operate a mounted rotary switch controlling the current to

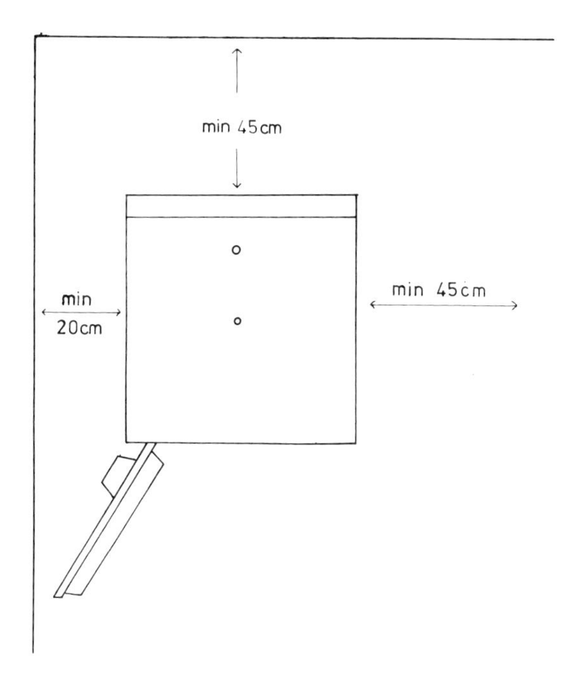

96. Plan showing the ideal siting of a kiln in a studio with minimum spacing distances

the kiln. The key cannot be removed from this rotary switch until the current is switched off, thus making it impossible to open the kiln door while the current is on. In countries where there are not statutory regulations governing the safety of kilns, it is wise to have a door safety switch fitted which switches off the current as the door is opened.

7. Firing capacity? Electric kilns are supplied in two firing ranges, up to 1200°C maximum and up to 1300°C maximum. As with the question of size, it is better to pay the small amount extra for the higher firing range so that stoneware temperatures can be reached if necessary.

8. Siting the kiln? It is important to have a solid foundation so that there is no possibility of the kiln being even a little unstable. If it shakes when the door is shut after loading, it is possible that movement of the shelves, props or pots will lead to disasters such as several pots being stuck together or a whole shelf collapsing on to the pots beneath. The kiln must be sited with at least 45cm space to the rear so that there is easy access for servicing and repair, and at least 20cm from the wall on the door-opening side. It is also preferable that the kiln be sited away from clay storage areas so that the heat will not dry out the clay.

9. Maintenance? Some suppliers provide a maintenance and repair service, and this must be taken into consideration when deciding where to place an order.

Kiln Furniture

Some suppliers of kilns also supply packs of furniture suited to each type of kiln. If, however, furniture has to be ordered separately, the following points should be taken into consideration.

Shelves, sometimes listed as 'bats', are made in various grades designed for use at different temperatures. Decide what maximum temperature is to be reached and order accordingly. It is better to break the line of shelves in a kiln so that the heat circulates freely; this is done by the use of half- and quarter-shelves, which also allows the kiln to be used to capacity, since smaller shelves can be built around awkward and bulky pots rather than leaving empty spaces. Two or three full-sized and several each of half- and quarter-shelves should be ordered. We have, over the years, cut up a number of shelves in order to pack particular kilns, and we find that the resultant odd sizes and shapes are in constant use.

Shelf supports, generally listed as 'props', can be purchased as straight pillars or with castellations. They can be used with round discs as tops or bases to provide stability, but these tend to take up a lot of room just where an awkwardly shaped pot would fit in, and with careful loading they are not

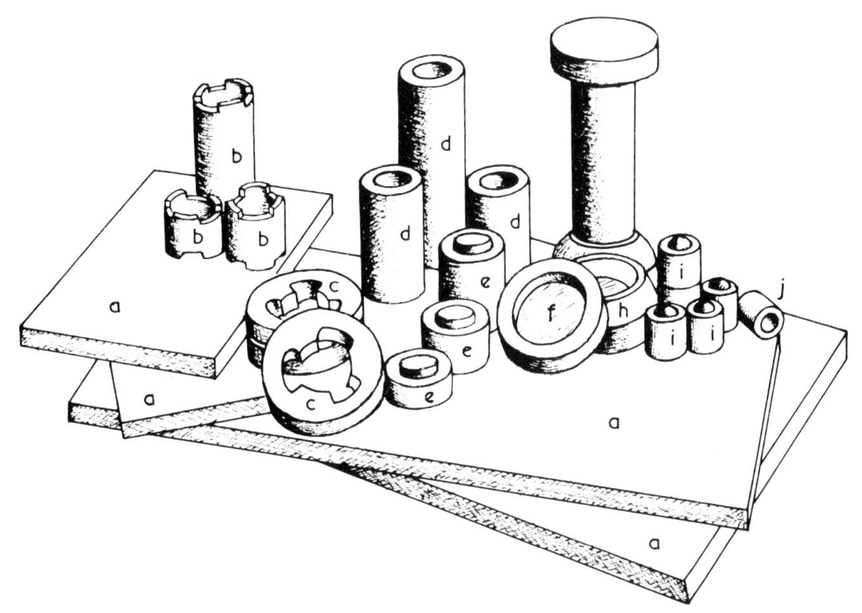

97. Kiln furniture used in the Camperdown Pottery, as supplied by Podmore & Sons Ltd: *a* kiln shelves (bats); *b* interlocking castellated props; *c* circular discs for use with castellated props; *d* tubular props; *e* interlocking extensions for use with tubular props or alone; *f, h* collar and base support for use with tubular props; *i* domed and recessed props, interlocking; *j* props recessed at both ends for top of pillar

really essential. They are, however, invaluable where a single pillar of props can be fitted between other ware and, by using a disc on top of the pillar, a small shelf can be fitted into a space which would otherwise have to remain unused. For larger shelves we use castellated props in two heights, 1in and 1½in, with a diameter of 1¾in. For the smaller, lighter shelves we use domed and recessed props of 1in diameter and 1in high, with some recessed at both ends to form the tops of the pillars. We find the castellated props are excellent for stability and more economical of space in the kiln than tubular props with collars and base supports.

Stilts and spurs are used as supports for earthenware during glost firing if it is glazed on the base or if the glaze is likely to flux to any great extent. They must not be used for stoneware as they distort at temperatures above 1200°C.

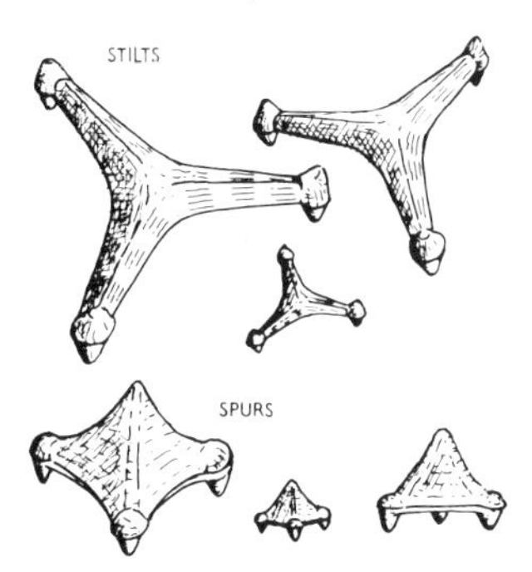

98. Stilts and spurs

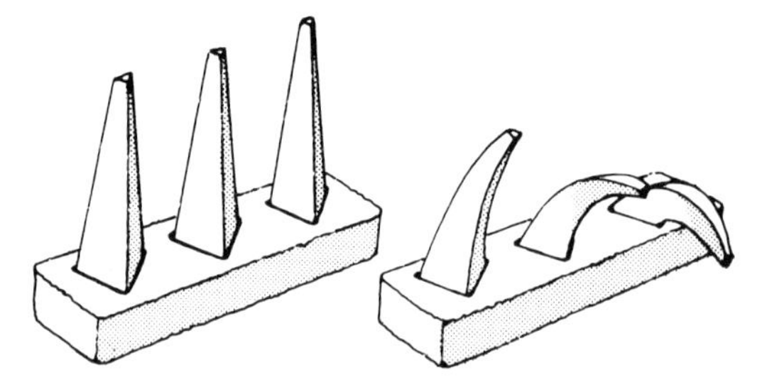

99. Staffordshire cones as supplied by Fulham Pottery. *Left*: ready for use. *Right*: appearance after a perfect firing

There are three sizes of spur and seven sizes of stilt available, and if economy is a consideration it is better to take advantage of those firms which supply packs of 100 assorted stilts or spurs. We have found that spurs are more convenient to use than stilts as they can be placed in groups of three or more, making it easier to place irregularly shaped work and obtain stability. They are also cheaper, and less easily broken than the stilt with its long points.

Pyrometric cones, which are heat-work indicators, must be used if the kiln has no control panel or heat indicator. They are made from ceramic materials which are sensitive to heat over a period of time, and are designed to bend at a certain temperature after a defined period of heating. Three consecutive grades of cones are used for each firing: the lowest anticipates the completion of the firing, the second indicates that the optimum temperature has been reached, and the third acts as a check for overfiring. It is advisable to place cones in a number of strategic positions throughout the kiln on the first few firings, whether a control panel is in use or not, to ascertain where any 'hot spots' occur, as there is always a certain amount of variation in temperature within the kiln.

The cones should be set at a slight angle in a stand supplied for the purpose or in a support made from a body such as sculpting marl, dried well before use, and so positioned in the kiln that they can be observed through the spyhole without difficulty. To test the placing of the cones, put a small torch on the shelf beside them before closing the door and look through the spyhole. They must be clearly visible just in front of the hole, otherwise they will merge into the background as everything takes on the colour characteristic of the temperature.

The use of pyrometric cones is usually described very thoroughly in suppliers' catalogues, but basically the procedure is as follows. When the estimated duration of firing is nearly over, a watch should be kept on the cones; when the first one begins to bend, a regular check every five minutes is advisable. When the tip of the second cone is level with the base, the kiln should be switched off. The temperature at which this position is reached is known as the 'squatting temperature'. The third cone should be almost unaffected, showing that the kiln has not overfired.

There are several makes of cone on the market with slightly differing squatting temperatures, and it is essential to use the cones which match the maturing temperatures of the glazes chosen.

Protection of shelves. Some suppliers list 'bat washes', which are generally a combination of china clay and flint mixed with water. These are painted on to the shelves to prevent pots sticking during a glost firing when the bases are not glazed and no stilts are being used. They also protect the shelves from possible drips of glaze. We always use a fine silica sand rather than a bat wash for both earthenware and stoneware firing. This proves very economical as it can be rubbed off with a carborundum stone after each firing, sieved to remove any glaze-contaminated lumps, and re-used for as long as it remains clean. However, great care must be taken not to spread any of the sand on to the elements in an electric kiln or brush it into pots on lower shelves.

Carborundum slip stone. It is essential to have a good slip stone in any pottery, for cleaning off kiln shelves and removing stilt marks from the bottoms of pots after firing.

10 Loading, Firing and Unloading Kilns

We are convinced that all pottery students who are physically capable should be taught to load and fire kilns as well as to make and glaze pots. They should be encouraged to take the responsibility of handling other people's work when loading and not to give up if things go wrong. A great deal can be learned through making mistakes, and these lessons are not easily forgotten. We start by teaching how to unload, so that students can gain confidence in the handling of pots and learn how they are placed within the kiln.

We cool our kiln rapidly after firing to keep work moving through the studio. We find that if a biscuit kiln is fired to 900°C overnight, the plug taken out at 8am and the door cracked open at 9am, the kiln can be unloaded between 10 and 11am, depending on how tightly it was packed. The pots are then glazed as soon as they are cool enough and loaded back into the still warm kiln for firing the same day. We unload earthenware glost fired to 1080°C about eight hours after the kiln has switched off, which enables a night firing to be unloaded by the following afternoon class. The stoneware glost we generally leave overnight to cool.

The following are the instructions given to our students for use with our kiln, which has a West QAL automatic temperature (indicating) controller with thermocouple, cut-off/control selection switch and time switch.

100. Carol Jones, sculpting-marl crocodile, 52cm long

Unloading

1. Switch off the kiln at the main switch as soon as possible after 'cut-out'. This is essential from a safety point of view, because otherwise the kiln will refire again on a twenty-four-hour cycle governed by the time switch.
2. Remove the plug from the top of the kiln, first making sure that there is room on top of the kiln to put it down, as it can be very hot.

3. The kiln door should be opened slightly (cracked open) when the temperature has fallen to 400°C. To test the temperature, switch on the main switch and press the centre (reset) button. The temperature will then register on the indicating dial. Switch off at the main switch immediately the temperature is noted.

4. Unload the kiln at 200°C or below.

5. Use a thick *dry* cloth over the hands to lift the pieces out if the kiln is still hot. If the cloth is damp, severe scalding can result from the steam which is generated through contact with the hot pottery.

6. The ware at the bottom of the kiln will cool before that at the top, so if possible unload from the bottom; as space occurs, move pots down from the upper shelves so that they may cool within the kiln until they are fit to handle safely. This is particularly important in a glost kiln as sudden changes in temperature may cause the glaze to craze.

7. Place the ware on metal cake grids or similar racks to enable air to circulate freely round the pieces, allowing even cooling and avoiding possible spoiling of work surfaces.

8. Remove shelves carefully, keeping them level. Use an initial upward lift, holding the front edge with both hands, fingers underneath and thumbs on top. This allows any props which have stuck to the shelf to be detected before it is removed. A great deal of damage can be done if a pillar of props is knocked against pots on the shelf below, or if the prop which had stuck drops off when the shelf is halfway out of the kiln. Each shelf must be cleaned off with a carborundum stone, which removes the sand and any slivers of stilt or glaze. These slivers are exceedingly sharp, and if any attempt is made to wipe the sand from a shelf using bare hands the resulting cuts can be very deep and painful.

9. Stand props and shelves taken from the warm kiln in a place where they will not damage floor coverings or table tops. Unless the floor of the pottery is of stone or concrete, it is a good idea to have a spare shelf or piece of asbestos laid flat on the floor on which to stand the hot furniture and shelves. A strong asbestos sheet fitted as a shelf beneath the kiln is an ideal place to store furniture. Shelves must be stored standing on edge; if they are laid flat, any which have warped are likely to break under the weight of the others.

10. Stone off the bottom of glost ware to remove any sand, glaze or stilt, as these can cause damage to furniture as well as hands.

11. Make sure that the kiln elements are free from sand or fragments of clay before reloading. It is a good idea to use a vacuum cleaner with a small nozzle to clean the seating of the elements of an electric kiln; this avoids disturbing the elements, which become very brittle after they have been heated and are easily broken.

Loading a Biscuit Kiln

1. Always make sure that the raw green ware is thoroughly dried out before firing it. One way to do this is to stand it on top of the kiln during the previous firing.
2. Green ware is very fragile when dry and should be handled with care. Take the weight with both hands beneath each piece. Never hold an unfired pot by a handle or rim.
3. Start loading into a warm kiln if possible. All types of clay can be fired together in a biscuit kiln, but care must be taken not to put red earthenware pots touching light-coloured ones, as the red can stain the lighter clay.
4. Pots can be loaded inside or on top of one another, but weight must be considered, so that light pieces are placed on top of heavy ones, and clearance should be allowed for shrinkage during firing. Never place a pot made from a body with a low shrinkage inside one with a higher rate of shrinkage. The pots should be placed not less than a finger's width from the elements.
5. Use as few shelves as possible, as every shelf is a waste of room and absorbs heat energy. Three pillars of props are more stable than four, and take up less kiln space.
6. Shelves need not be protected with sand or bat wash for firing biscuit ware.
7. Shut the kiln door very gently to avoid jogging or displacing the contents.
8. Make sure that the plug is not in the top of the kiln so that steam can escape during the initial drying process.

101. Anita Wolfe, terracotta children, 18cm maximum

102. Control panel as supplied by Cromartie Kilns Ltd

Setting the Kiln for Biscuit Firing

1. Disengage the time clock by unscrewing its centre knob.
2. Adjust the set point indicator to 200°C, using the knob to the right of the dial which is concealed by a small hinged flap. Set the heat input regulator to 10, put the upper switch to 'control' and the lower (main) switch to 'on', and press the reset button. The kiln should now be working—switching on for ten seconds and off for fifty seconds. If it does not switch on, the time switch is still in control from a previous firing; in this case, the small red button on the side of the time clock should be pressed and the reset button pressed again.
3. Leave the kiln working at this ratio until there is no steam coming from the plug hole. Test by holding a mirror over the hole. If no moisture is being driven off, the mirror will not mist over. This drying process may take several hours, especially if the kiln is tightly packed and heavy pieces are included.
4. When no moisture is evident at 200°C (this is the temperature at which

water molecules that have been combined within the clay are released), alter the set point to 900°C, the top switch to 'cut out' and the heat input regulator tò 100.

5. Put the plug in the top of the kiln very gently. The kiln will then fire safely to 900°C and switch off.

6. If, as in our studio, cheaper night-tariff power is available, then the time clock should be put in control. The drying process should be carried out during the day and the time switch set once it is complete. At 200°C and with the plug in place, the kiln will lose little heat over several hours and will fire safely when the time clock switches it on.

If a night firing is required, set the time clock as follows:

a Switch off at the lower (main) switch.

b Set time switch 'on' pointer to the appropriate time on the clock (this cannot be done unless the centre knob on the clock is undone) and the 'off' pointer to about two hours after the estimated completion of the firing.

A biscuit kiln takes approximately eight hours to complete firing to 900°C. Allowances should be made in the timing if the kiln is particularly tightly packed or if there are large heavy articles present which will absorb a lot of heat energy. Setting the clock to switch off after the expected duration of the firing provides a safety measure against the failure of the pyrometer (instrument for measuring high temperatures).

c Tighten the centre knob of the clock and replace the clock cover. This engages the clock and the switch.

d Set the main switch to 'on'.

e Press the reset button.

f Press the time switch control button which is on the side of the clock. This should cause the kiln to switch on. Press it again to switch off the kiln, leaving the clock in control.

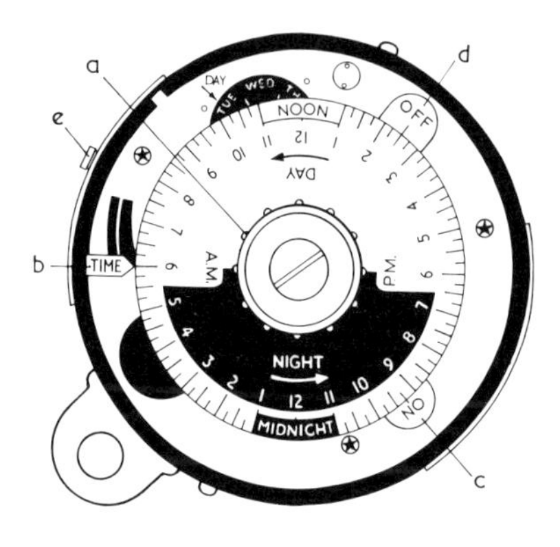

103. Sangamo Weston time switch as supplied by Cromartie Kilns Ltd: *a* centre screw knob; *b* time indicator; *c* 'switch on' pointer; *d* 'switch off' pointer; *e* red control button

Loading a Glost Kiln

1. A bat wash or sand must be applied to all shelves used for a glost firing. The sand should be smoothed over the shelves, using a carborundum stone, before they are placed in an electric kiln, to reduce the chances of sand being brushed on to the elements. The advantage of sand over a bat wash is that it can easily be completely removed, so that both sides of a shelf can be used; the shelves will bend slightly on each glost firing, and the use of alternate sides will correct the warping.

2. Glaze will easily rub off before it is fired, so all pots should be handled as little as possible, resting the pot on the hands rather than gripping it with the fingers. The hands should be wiped with a dry cloth before handling a different glaze. If oxides have been fingered or painted over the raw glaze the pot should, if possible, be lifted by spreading the fingers inside it, supporting the weight with the fingers of the other hand underneath. Particular care must be taken not to smudge painting which has been done using overglaze colours.

3. Sort out the ware to be fired before starting to load, making sure that all the pieces are to be fired to the same temperature. (Different earthenware bodies can be fired together as long as the glazes used all mature at the same temperature.) Mistakes at this stage can be serious. Earthenware, if overfired, will be grossly distorted, while the shelves and furniture will be spoilt by the melted glaze and the fusion of the clay to anything with which it is in contact. Stoneware in an earthenware kiln will be underfired, with the glaze almost unaltered, and will require firing again to the correct temperature—a costly waste of energy and kiln space.

Place the pieces in groups of similar height in order to work out the placing with the greatest economy of space and handling. For a first attempt at loading, it is best to set each shelf-full outside the kiln on a spare shelf to make sure the pots will fit safely within the space available. They should then be transferred to the kiln with the minimum of handling, keeping the same arrangement.

Tall pots should be placed at the top of the kiln to avoid the use of tall pillars of props, which are unstable. Moreover, the presence of a shelf immediately below the pyrometer can lead to the overfiring of the pots below it, as this shelf will shield the pyrometer from the rest of the kiln and slow the heating of the space around it.

4. When loading stoneware or placing earthenware on sand, check the bottom of each pot to make sure that it is free of glaze; stoneware must be free of glaze 5mm up the side of the pot.

5. Use stilts or spurs to support earthenware if it is glazed on the base or there is a possibility of the glaze from the sides running badly. Stilts must not be used for stoneware as they are not able to withstand stoneware tempera-

104. Slab pots. *Top left*: John Herbert, stoneware vase with textured surface, 20cm; stoneware bottle. *Top right*: Judy Cunningham-Smith, carved stoneware box with manganese oxide and rutile painted on to a transparent green glaze. *Bottom left*: Daphne Hunt, earthenware lamp base with textured top, copper oxide and rutile painted on to transparent glaze. *Bottom right*: Beryl Watts, Ikebana container, double-dipped; Carol Jones, earthenware jar with appliqué design

tures. If there is a possibility that the glaze may run, a stoneware pot should be placed on a small piece of shelf or a prop, with plenty of sand underneath to protect the shelf from drips of glaze.

6. When sand is used, each pot must be positioned without disturbing the sand. A pot which must be moved should be picked up and replaced. If it is pushed, the sand will heap up against the foot of the pot and stick to the glaze during firing.

7. Pots must be at least 1cm from one another and from the walls of the kiln. Do not place pieces less than 2.5cm from the pyrometer. We find that we load a glost kiln by feel rather than sight. The fingertip is a good guide to the distance between pots, but it must be used carefully so as not to disturb the glaze. It is easy to slip the hand gently round behind a pot to check the distance while placing; this prevents wastage of space due to overcautious-

ness—and, of course, the wastage of materials which occurs when pots placed too close become fused together.

8. If possible, break the line of shelves to allow good circulation of heat within the kiln. We try not to use more than two full shelves at a time, but make full use of the space available by using a lot of halves, quarters and odd sizes.

9. Before placing a shelf over pots within the kiln, test that there is at least 5mm clearance above the tallest pot by gently laying a batten across the props. If a full-sized prop will give more clearance than is necessary, then to save wastage of space small pieces of thin shelving can be used instead. When the shelf has been placed in position, the clearance should be checked visually to ensure that it is sufficient to allow for warping of the shelf.

10. Close the door very gently to avoid disturbing the contents of the kiln.

11. Check that the plug is not in the top of the kiln.

Setting the Kiln for Glost Firing

1. Disengage the time clock by unscrewing the centre knob on the clock.
2. Adjust the set point to the required temperature. This will vary according to the maturing temperature of the glazes used. Different bodies will need glazes of differing composition in order to obtain a good 'fit'—equality of expansion and contraction between body and glaze—which means that it is unrealistic to try to give any instructions regarding the correct firing temperature. However, a rough guideline to the two ranges of temperature can be given. Earthenware is generally fired between 1000°C and 1180°C; stoneware fires between 1200°C and 1250°C.
3. Set the heat input regulator to 100.
4. Put the upper switch to 'cut out'.
5. Put the main switch to 'on'.
6. Press the reset button. The kiln should now be firing. If it is not, the time switch is still in control. Disengage the switch by pressing the button on the side of the clock, and press the reset button again.
7. When the temperature has reached 200°C, gently put the plug in. This *must* be done gently to avoid knocking dust or fragments of firebrick into the pots in the kiln.
8. If the kiln is to complete the firing overnight using the time switch, the procedure described for setting the clock and timing mechanism for the biscuit kiln should be followed. Firing times for a glost kiln of the size we use depend on the voltage available and how tightly the kiln is loaded. Earthenware firing to 1075°C takes between ten and twelve hours. Stoneware firing to 1225°C takes between twelve and fifteen hours.

If the kiln is in the charge of more than one person, as is often the case in a communal workshop or school, it is a good idea to have a blackboard available on which the course of the firing can be laid out and any instructions to others can be written clearly so that they are not missed.

If the kiln has no input regulator or control for switching off, life is much more difficult and each firing is a major event demanding much attention and taking up a lot of the potter's time. In our own pre-control-panel days, there was far more excitement connected with each firing; instead of technical accessories such as pyrometers, heat input regulators and time switches, we had only the unreliable human eye trying to see a cone through a spyhole, often at some ridiculous time in the early hours before dawn. The kiln without automatic controls has to be switched on and off manually during the drying process until a temperature of 200°C is reached. Pyrometric cones have to be used to gauge the temperature; these must be watched closely when the firing is estimated to be nearly over, and the kiln switched off at the time indicated by the bending of the cones.

11 Glaze Composition and Preparation

Glaze is a form of glass covering which is applied to biscuit ware to increase its water-holding properties and to add decoration. Suppliers of ceramic materials list in their catalogues many colours and types of glaze which are specifically prepared to fit the bodies supplied by them. If one is purchasing ready-mixed glazes, it is essential to obtain both clay and glaze from the same supplier. It is very unlikely that any bought glaze will fit a locally dug and prepared clay. Some firms give detailed advice in their catalogues on the use of materials for the making of glaze. Fulham Pottery, Harrison Mayer and Podmore's are particularly thorough in this respect.

Since the Safety at Work Act of 1974 there are very few places in the United Kingdom where raw lead glazes may be used. Low-solubility lead bisilicate glazes may be used in schools, but satisfactory results may be obtained with less toxic lime-based glazes.

An economic way of obtaining variety of colour and texture is to purchase transparent basic glazes for earthenware and stoneware, together with small amounts of various colouring oxides and basic materials with which the glaze may be modified. The suppliers' catalogues are very helpful in this respect, as they give percentages for additions and details of the general effect of such additions to certain types of glaze. The following list gives a rough guide to the more commonly used compounds and the sort of effects produced by their use.

105. Mollie Herbert, coiled bird bath, 32cm

Bentonite—A natural colloidal clay formed by the weathering of volcanic ash, used to prevent glaze settling out when not in use. It must be added to the dry powdered glaze and not to the liquid. Two per cent by weight may be added to all glazes to aid suspension.
Boro-calcite, colemanite—a natural fritt (see page 117) acting as a good flux. It can sometimes produce a certain amount of opalescence and, in large quantities, a broken mottled surface.
Dolomite—a natural stone containing calcium and magnesium, generally used as a flux at high temperatures. Used in conjunction with other fluxes, it can be effective at temperatures as low as 1060°C. Used in quantities of over 5 per cent it begins to produce opacity, and in greater quantities can give a matt surface.
Feldspars—natural fritts used as the main ingredient for most glazes. Potash feldspar is used as the basis for most stoneware glazes, and gives a more durable product than the other feldspars. Soda feldspar makes a glaze with a lower maturing temperature than potash, and is thus more suitable for earthenware glazes. It is also used in the making of ash glazes. Nepheline syenite is a feldspar with a considerably lower silica content than the others in common use. It can be used to lower the melting point and to brighten the colour of a glaze.
Rutile—an impure form of titanium which gives a milky flecked effect; when used in conjunction with metallic oxides, it can produce some remarkable colour runs.
Strontium carbonate—a strong flux which can be used as an alternative to lead in low-firing glaze, and is used to improve glaze fit as it promotes a better glaze/body interaction.
Talc, French chalk—a hydrated magnesium silicate which can be used to cure crazing (cracking of the glaze) caused by excessive shrinkage. In large quantities it can be used to give a vellum-finish opaque glaze.
Tin oxide—a useful opacifier which gives an excellent white glaze but is very expensive.
Whiting—the main source of calcium in glazes. It acts as a high-temperature flux and promotes durability. In large quantities it can produce a matt effect.
Zirconium silicate—generally used as an opacifier instead of tin. Best results are obtained when it is used in conjunction with calcium or magnesium compounds. With lead it gives a cream colour. It should not be used as a direct substitute for tin in a recipe.
Chromium oxide—a highly toxic oxide which is not really worth using unless fired in a reducing atmosphere in conjunction with lead glazes, in which case pinks and reds can be obtained.
Cobalt oxide—a very strong colouring agent giving a rather hard blue unless used in very small quantities or in conjunction with other oxides. This is the basic ingredient of a black glaze. Up to 1 per cent can be used in a glaze;

106. Rene East, earthenware doodle, double-dipped, 20cm

more than this may cause bleeding and blackening of the glaze surface, giving it the appearance of badly burnt toast.

Copper oxide—used to produce greens in lead glazes and with calcium and magnesium. At high temperatures under oxidising conditions the colour tends to weaken considerably, so it is not recommended as a colourant for stoneware firing in an electric kiln. Especially good results can be obtained by using copper in conjunction with rutile.

Iron oxides—black, red, yellow ochre and crocus martis are the four commonly used oxides of iron. Most clay bodies contain a certain amount of iron oxide which gives the fired body its characteristic colour. This can range from pale cream to very dark brown, depending on the form of the oxide and the quantity present. Under reducing conditions greens and greys are produced. When added to glaze, iron oxide acts as a flux, even quite small amounts increasing the fluidity of a glaze quite considerably. The colour obtained depends ultimately on the temperature at which the glaze is fired and the type of atmosphere within the kiln. Red iron oxide and yellow ochre give yellow-browns (honey glazes), particularly when used with lead. Yellow ochre is the weaker of the two. Crocus martis and black iron oxide give dark browns with speckles. They are used with cobalt and manganese to give a black.

Manganese oxide—used with iron and cobalt to give a good black. In non-lead high-alkaline glazes a purple-brown colour is produced, especially when tin is present.

There are other colouring oxides, but these are better left alone until one is more experienced in the art of making up recipes, as they are either very expensive or difficult to use successfully without scientific calculation and accurate weighing.

When modifying a glaze with colouring agents, it is best to make small experimental batches and to keep a very careful record of all measurements and of the firing conditions. In this way even the 'accidental' discovery can be repeated.

If you wish to make glazes from the basic ingredients, it is better to get a good book on the subject and to study the chemistry of the process than to rely on guesswork. The recipes that can be found in most general books on pottery-making can lead to wastage, as the favourite glazes of the authors are designed to fit certain bodies, and it is more than likely that the body you wish to glaze has nothing like the same properties. If this is the case, a certain amount of modification is necessary in order to obtain a fit and to produce the desired colour, and this modification cannot be done economically without a good understanding of the physical and chemical properties of glazes and their constituents. The large number of tests necessary to obtain a good fit from a chemically stable glaze are likely to prove very expensive without a prior knowledge of what will not work.

Glazes can be produced economically by the use of ash, which contains all the ingredients of a glaze, although not necessarily in the correct proportions. The addition of simple raw materials such as soda feldspar and flint can give rewarding and fascinating results.

The ash can be obtained from wood fuel used in domestic heating or the firing of kilns, or from straw, vegetable matter or wood burnt in a bonfire. The composition of the ash varies considerably from plant to plant, and even ash from a single species can differ from place to place according to the

107. Carved bowls. *Left*: Ruth Rocket, transparent glaze with dark glaze painted on relief pattern. *Right*: Jane Jackson, dark-glazed exterior wiped off to leave glaze in the carving, then dipped into transparent glaze, 20cm diameter

mineral content of the ground on which the plant has grown. It is important that the ash is pure, without coal or coke ash included, and if it is collected from a bonfire, care must be taken to exclude any soil. The presence of these impurities in any quantity could increase the maturing temperature to above the normal stoneware firing range.

It is wise to collect a large quantity of ash before making tests so that, once a satisfactory formula is discovered, a useful amount of glaze can be made before it becomes necessary to experiment with a new batch of ash.

When sufficient ash has been collected it should be cleaned and, preferably, washed. It is possible to use ash that has merely been sieved to remove particles and lumps of charcoal and unburnt matter, but this has the disadvantage that the potassium carbonate present, although it produces interesting effects, will render the glaze caustic, causing damage to skin and clothing during use. The safest procedure is to wash the ash several times to remove the soluble potash. First, half fill a bucket with water and carefully add ash until it is nearly full—a plastic bucket is best as it will not be harmed by the caustic solution. Stir well and allow the heavy ash to settle. Skim off any floating particles using a plastic sieve, and ladle or siphon off the water as the ash settles. Top up with fresh water and skim again if necessary. Repeat this process until the water no longer feels 'soapy'. Four or five changes of water will usually be sufficient. Pass the washed ash through a 30 mesh sieve, having ground up any fused lumps in a mortar, and spread it on polythene to dry, then crush the dried cake of ash to a powder ready for use.

Before making any additions to the ash, always fire a sample of it to the temperature at which the glaze is to mature to determine whether it is underfiring and needs the addition of a suitable flux, or overfiring and requires additions of clay, talc or flint.

When making up glazes, it is essential to the chemical balance that nothing is lost. Some of the ingredients will pass through the sieve with ease, and some will stick to everything they touch. If the minimum of water is used to mix the glaze, then everything may be washed down thoroughly and the washing water sieved and used to make up the batch to the required consistency. In this way the absolute minimum is wasted and, as long as all the tools are always clean at the start, the glaze can be repeated very accurately, since the exact formula of the batch is known—no little bits of this and that creeping in from a dirty brush and either spoiling a complete batch of glaze or creating a wonderful new effect which cannot be repeated without very complicated chemical analysis in a laboratory.

We keep a large bottle into which we put any glaze cleaned from the bottoms of pots and any oxides left over from decorating and contaminated with glaze. When the bottle is full, we sieve the contents and add water to make up a glaze; thus no glaze or oxides are wasted. These 'scrapings' glazes are often very special, and are of course unrepeatable. There is only one rule for the use of these 'economy' glazes: *do not use on pottery where they will be in contact with food or water.* This is because such glazes may be unstable, and toxic substances may be released when they come into contact with food.

Cobalt oxide is such a strong colouring agent that its presence will make the scrapings glazes blue. To avoid this, it is a good idea to have two jars and to keep scrapings containing cobalt oxide separate from the others.

Preparation of Glaze for Use

For the preparation of a glaze, the following items are needed:

2 gallon bowl
2 gallon bucket
Medium-coarse sieve (60 mesh)
Fine sieve (100 mesh)
Flat wooden stirrer, 3cm wide and about 35cm long
Two 2cm wide flat wooden battens
3cm lawn brush or strong paintbrush
Supply of clean water
Small clean sponge or piece of clean plastic foam
Palette knife (thin flexible kitchen knife) or rubber kidney
Scales for weighing dry ingredients

1. Weigh all the dry ingredients into the bucket and mix well.
2. Place the battens across the bowl and rest the medium-coarse sieve on them.
3. Press the dry ingredients, a little at a time, through the sieve into the bowl. If there are no toxic substances present this can be done with the fingers, but otherwise a palette knife or rubber kidney should be used. This takes time and energy but is well worth the effort, as it makes the mixed paste easy to sieve.
4. Rinse out the bucket with a little clean water and add the rinsings to the dry ingredients in the bowl.
5. If necessary, add more clean water to the bowl to make the mix into a fairly thick paste.
6. Put the battens and the fine sieve, upside down, on the top of the bucket. Brush the paste through the sieve into the bucket.
7. Wash the sieves, tools and brush in the bowl, using a little clean water and the sponge. Pass the washings through the fine sieve into the bucket. Do not use too much water for washing or the glaze will be made too thin.
8. If necessary, add more clean water to the glaze mix in order to obtain the correct consistency. This will vary according to the type of glaze, but a

good guide is the glaze remaining on the stirrer after the mix has been stirred; it should coat the wood well but not thickly. Transparent glazes are generally thinner than opaque ones. Remember that it is easier to add water than to remove it.

9. Wipe down the sides of the bucket to the level of the glaze, using the sponge. Dry glaze falling into the batch will make it lumpy, and it will then need to be resieved.

10. The glaze should not be used for at least a day after it has been mixed, to allow it to mature and to give the small bubbles formed during the sieving process time to rise to the surface and burst. If a pot is dipped while they are still present, they will prevent proper coverage by the glaze.

11. Wash all the sieves and tools properly and make sure that a proper written record of the batch has been made.

12 Decoration of Fired Ware

The glazing and decoration of a pot can make or mar it, and therefore great thought and care should be given to the choice and application of glaze and any other decoration.

The following are the methods we teach.

108. Judy Cunningham-Smith, coiled and tooled doodle with fingered oxide decoration, 12cm

Glazing

Articles used for glazing are:

A table, separate from the general workbench to avoid contamination of the glazes
A stirrer, which can be purpose-made or a simple wooden batten
A ladle and a slip trailer
A small fine-textured sponge or piece of plastic foam
Two jugs
A small bowl (we use plastic margarine pots or cream cartons)
A wire cake tray or similar rack
A soft, long-haired brush, listed as a 'flat duster' in the suppliers' catalogues
A large bowl over which to glaze big or awkward pots
A whirler
A large lidded jar to contain scrapings and contaminated glaze and in which to wash brushes containing glaze or oxides

1. First collect the items needed for the glazing of the pot in question.
2. Check that everything is clean, including the table, as spilt glaze can be mopped up and saved if it is clean. Rinse the sponge, which can look clean on the outside while retaining a mass of clay or other matter inside.
3. Having decided which glaze is to be used, take the bucket (or bowl) of glaze carefully to the table, making sure that the glaze in it is not disturbed.
4. Some glazes settle out considerably when left standing, while others stay in suspension, leaving only a thin film of water on the surface. In either case this water must not be discarded.

Gently tip the bucket a little, and either ladle the excess clear water from the top of the glaze or, if there is very little, use a slip trailer. Put one ladleful into a small bowl and the rest, if any, into a jug. If the studio is shared, it is wise to remove all the water from the glaze before stirring, as there is a very real danger that someone else may have added water to it by accident or design. If the glaze is stirred and found to be too thin, it is necessary to wait for it to settle out again before any more water can be removed.

5. Stir the glaze well, making sure that all the sediment is mixed in from the bottom and round the sides of the container. Some glazes settle out into a comparatively hard mass which is difficult to break up. In this case, a metal knife or spoon is useful for cutting into the mass. Once the lumps are lifted from the bottom they will rapidly break up.

109. Slip trailers

6. If necessary, return water from the jug until the glaze is of the required consistency. This can only be judged by experience and intuition, but, as stated above, a good guide is the way in which the glaze coats the stirrer. It should cover it well but not too thickly. Porosity of bodies, firing temperatures of the biscuit ware, different glaze compositions and the possibility of double-dipping all have to be taken into consideration when judging how thick the glaze should be.
7. Brush any surface dust off the pot to be glazed. Do this away from the glazing table, preferably outside, to cut down on dust in the studio.
8. Work out how to hold the pot so that it can be dipped easily and with as little handling as possible. Remember that the wrist will not bend backwards easily while holding something, and that it is very easy to trap air within the pot, which will prevent part of it being glazed properly. Small pots should be dipped and turned a little so that the inside is completely covered. Larger

pots can be dealt with by filling a jug with glaze, using it to fill the pot about one-third full, and then quickly tipping the surplus back from the pot into the bucket while turning the pot to ensure that the whole of the inside is covered. The outside can then be glazed. First, remove any runs from the outside, using the sponge dipped in the bowl of water. Fill the jug with glaze and place the bucket or bowl on a whirler. Place a grid over the container and stand the pot on it, upside down if possible. The outside can then be glazed by pouring the glaze quickly over the pot, turning the container so that no part is missed. If this is not done quickly enough the glaze first applied will be dry before the application is finished and a second layer will stick to the dry coating, producing an uneven texture and colour in the fired glaze. This will not spoil all glazes, but transparent or white opaque glazes tend to look very streaky and unattractive if this happens.

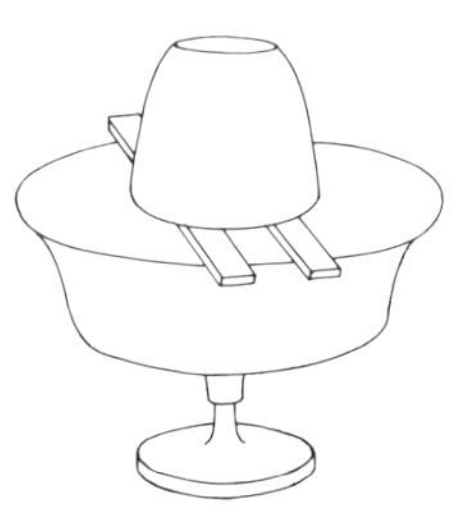

110. Large pot ready for glazing over a bowl on a whirler

9. Practise the appropriate movements needed for the process and give the glaze a final stir. The heaviest ingredients will have started to settle out almost immediately. Dip the fingertips with which the pot is to be held into the glaze, and then proceed with glazing. The application should be carried out as quickly as possible, as the longer the pot is in the glaze the more it will absorb, it becomes saturated with water, the glaze will then start to wash off again, and the pot will have to be cleaned and dried out before it can be reglazed. Do not worry about small 'misses', as these can be filled in later using a soft brush.

10. Place the pot on a grid, touching it as little as possible. The glaze will pull off if touched while still wet.

11. As soon as the glaze is dry, touch up any misses and fingermarks, using a soft brush filled with glaze and applying it with a single dab. If you try to paint glaze on to the pot as though painting a wall, the glaze will tend to be removed rather than applied. When it is dry, any uneven ridges and runs can be removed by gently rubbing them with a dry finger. You can tell when the glaze is dry because it looks powdery and much lighter than when wet.

12. If no stilts are to be used, sponge off or scrape the glaze from the bottom of the pot. If double-dipped or stoneware, clean 5mm up the side of the pot as well. Use the spare water in the bowl for sponging off. Scrape with a straight-bladed knife, collecting the glaze on a sheet of paper and placing it in the scrapings jar.

13. Still using the water taken from the top of the glaze, wash off the stirrer and any other tools used. Sponge down the inside of the bucket and return the washings and any spare water left in the jug to the glaze. If the washings have become contaminated, they should be put in the scrapings jar to avoid spoiling the glaze, but not thrown away.
14. Wash all tools thoroughly in clean water and put them away.

On-glaze Decoration

Double Dipping
One of the most attractive forms of glaze decoration is produced by double dipping. The reaction between the two glazes gives the effect of life and depth through fluxing and crawling. The same effect would not be obtained if the two glazes were mixed together before they were applied to the pot.

A white opaque underglaze with a darker glaze applied over it generally gives very good results, especially if the second one contains copper, titanium or manganese. We often use scrapings glazes in this way, but it must always be remembered that these must not be used on articles which will come into contact with food.

The first application of glaze must be completely dry before the pot is dipped into the second glaze, and it is very important that the wet glaze is not touched, as the contact will either pull the glaze off or mix the two layers, producing an unpleasant mark. For this reason, it is advisable to check that the pot can be easily held by its foot or that the whole pot can be covered by pouring before deciding to double-dip.

111. Judy Cunningham-Smith, double-dipped coiled stoneware vase. The coils were pulled down with a fingertip on the outside and left as decoration

Thin ware is very difficult to double-dip, as it cannot absorb all the water from the two applications. On very thin edges the glaze will tend to crawl away towards the thicker areas of clay.

Painting Glaze over an Unfired Base Glaze

We keep small jars of each of our glazes for painting over a base colour. This technique produces more subtle colouring than that produced by enamels or underglaze paints. The glaze is laid on to the base colour using a soft brush which will not pull the first layer off.

Allowing a second glaze to dribble down over the first is also very effective, as long as the second one fluxes easily so that the boundaries between the dribbles and the base are softened by the merging of the two. The pots of glaze must be kept clean and topped up with water as necessary, because they tend to become too thick very quickly as the water evaporates in the small jars. They must be stirred well every time a brushful is taken, and after use the brushes should be wiped out into the pots as well as possible and then washed in the water settled out in the current scrapings jar, or washed in a little clean water which can then be added to the scrapings.

112. Marny Millard, impressed stoneware jar built up with lumps. Coloured glazes painted on to a white base glaze, 23cm

Painting with Oxides over an Unfired Base Glaze

Painting oxides over a base glaze before firing produces beautiful colouring effects and is a way of obtaining great variation simply and economically. This is of great value if space and finance are limited.

The oxides are mixed with clean water in the proportions by volume of one part dry powdered oxide to six parts water. Only small amounts should be mixed at a time, and these can be kept in small screw-capped jars. The small quantities allow for a greater number of mixtures, and also if they become contaminated the wastage is not great. The jars should be clearly marked to show the contents. Experimentation can lead to the discovery of combinations personal to the individual potter, because very minor variations in the proportions can produce marked differences in the fired results. Different glaze compositions and firing temperatures will also cause variations in effect.

113. Mollie Herbert, pinched earthenware vase with coiled pinched-out neck. Oxide brushwork over white opaque glaze, 34cm

The powdered oxides are suspended in water, not dissolved. This means that they will settle out very rapidly, so the mixture must be stirred *every time the brush is dipped into it.* Shake or wipe off excess mixture into the jar and using light, quick strokes apply the oxide to the glazed surface. Do not try to spread the oxide in the manner used to paint a wall. Wait until the oxide is dry before touching up any gaps. Do not put on a second layer, as this will either pull off the glaze and first layer or produce a metallic bubbled patch which looks rather like badly burnt toast. This same effect is obtained all too easily if cobalt or copper oxide is applied thickly. Experience will show the correct strength for these. If you are in difficulty, the addition of a small amount of clear transparent glaze to the mixture may help.

This type of decoration can be used in several ways: a single all-over covering of oxide; several different oxides or mixtures in an all-over covering; bold patterns, possibly highlighting patterns in the clay; intricate designs.

We use many mixtures and single oxides, but find the following are the most popular.

Copper oxide over white opaque glaze produces pale green to black, depending on the thickness of the application.
Copper oxide over transparent glaze on red earthenware produces rich deep green to black.
Copper oxide and rutile over white opaque glaze produces rich green to black with pale highlights and runs, especially on pots with steep sides.
Copper oxide and rutile over transparent glaze on red earthenware produces a dark olive to black with paler highlights and runs.
Cobalt oxide over white opaque or transparent glaze on a light-coloured body produces a rather hard blue. This is effective if used in small quantities in conjunction with painted glazes or for making simple line decoration, as in the traditional blue and white majolica ware. Cobalt has a tendency to spread into the surrounding glaze during application, but this can be remedied to a certain extent by substituting a tannin solution such as strong tea or the liquor made by boiling oak bark for the water used to suspend the oxide. Cobalt can also be mixed with white opaque glaze or talc to soften and lighten the colour.
Manganese oxide and rutile over transparent glaze gives a beautiful effect, better seen than described, which varies with the colour of the body used. Over opaque white it gives a soft mottled brown.
Manganese oxide over transparent glaze on a red earthenware body gives a very dark rich brown. Over white opaque glaze it gives an unexceptional mid-brown. Sometimes gold flecks can be obtained by painting manganese oxide on to the raw earthenware body and then painting copper oxide over a transparent glaze for the glost firing.
Iron oxides when painted over glazes give a clear line without fluxing and mixing with the surrounding glaze, which makes them excellent for painting detail at earthenware temperatures. At stoneware temperatures they begin to flux and no longer give such a definite line.
Mixtures can give interesting effects if a stiff brush is used to flick different oxides on to a base application of glaze. This is especially good if rutile is used. An all-over covering of iron or copper oxide followed by flicking with rutile can give remarkable results.

All mixtures and single oxides can be painted or flicked on to any raw glaze, but the effects will vary with the composition of each glaze.

Fingered Oxides
A method of giving depth and variety of colour to a glaze is to 'finger' or smudge a mixture of dry powdered oxides on to the glazed pot before firing. We have done a considerable amount of research into this method of

decoration, as it is both economical and attractive. Only colourless transparent and white opaque glazes are necessary, but any glaze can be used.

As the oxides are far from evenly distributed over the surface, they interact with the glaze and with one another to differing extents, depending on the concentration of the oxides. More pleasing effects are possible using this method than can be obtained by applying a single-colour glaze. Some of the oxides are toxic, so it is very important to scrub the hands and fingernails thoroughly after employing this method of decoration.

114. Judy Cunningham-Smith, multiple square pin pot. Fingered oxides over white opaque glaze, 27cm

The oxides are used in the state in which they are purchased, with no further grinding. Measure the required proportions into a small clean screw-capped jar and shake gently to mix. The jars should be labelled and numbered to tally with test pieces.

The mixture is applied to the unfired glazed pot, which should be placed on a whirler so that it is easily accessible from all sides. The pot should stand on a sheet of paper. Shake a small quantity of the mixed oxide into the lid of the jar, pick up a little on the tip of a finger and press it on to the pot with a slight smudging action. Most of the oxide will stick to the glaze, but any falling on to the paper should be picked up and used. The aim should be to finish the decoration of the pot using the last of the oxide from the paper. That remaining in the lid can be returned to the jar. Any left on the paper is put into the scrapings jar; it must not be returned to the jar of mixed oxide, as it will be contaminated by glaze.

After making over six hundred test pieces in both stoneware and earthenware, and using transparent and white opaque glazes at both temperatures for each test, we selected forty mixes which gave exceptionally good results, and these we use constantly. A few of these are given below, but they will give different results over different glazes and in different firing conditions. It is a simple matter for the potter to concoct his own special recipes to suit the clays and glazes he uses; our recipes are given only as a guide to what sort of mixture is a success. Whatever experiments are made, records must be kept, as it is very wasteful trying to repeat a mix when the proportions are not known.

115. Pin pots. *Left*: Daphne Hunt. *Right*: Janet Saunders

a 1 part black copper oxide, 1 part fine rutile
b 2 parts cobalt oxide, 3 parts fine rutile
c 2 parts red iron oxide, 2 parts chrome oxide, 1 part tin oxide, 2 parts colemanite
d 7 parts colemanite, 3 parts red iron oxide
e 2 parts rutile, 2 parts colemanite, 1 part cobalt oxide

Underglaze Colours

These are prepared, finely ground pigments which give predictable and consistent colours. Some are intermixable so that a wider range of colours is possible. These colours are usually applied to the leather-hard clay before it is fired to biscuit temperature; the ware is then glazed with a colourless transparent glaze. The colours may also be painted on to biscuit-fired ware before it is glazed. In this case, they must be mixed with gum arabic to avoid contamination of the glaze if the pot is to be dipped, but it is likely that the pigment will cause rejection of the glaze. The rejection can be overcome by firing the ware to 600°C to harden the pigment on to the body before applying the glaze, but this is not economical unless the kiln is full for the extra firing, and is therefore rather inconvenient.

We find the easiest and most attractive way of using underglaze colours is to mix them with a little transparent or white opaque glaze—transparent gives a bright colour, opaque softens—and to paint them *over* the unfired glaze. The effect is to give natural colours which are more pleasing than the hard lines produced by direct application to the body. Because of the high cost of the pigments and the ease with which glazes can be used for painting, we use underglaze colours only for delicate work such as the birds shown in illustration 116 and the figure in illustration 5, bottom left.

Underglaze colours can be obtained in a great range of colours, some of which are very strong and will produce a blistering effect if applied too thickly. Only experiment can show the correct thickness, which will vary with the glaze used, but our method of mixing with glaze counteracts the blistering to a great extent. For the sake of economy we have a set of palettes into which very small amounts of the colours are placed, each one labelled with the numbers of the appropriate pigments. These can be wetted and used whenever necessary. As long as it remains uncontaminated, each batch can be added to as it runs out, thus avoiding washing away and wasting some of the pigment each time a colour is used. The proportion of glaze to pigment will vary with each colour, so there is no hard and fast rule which can be given here. The mixed pigment should be applied with very light, quick strokes of the brush to avoid pulling off any glaze or mixing the colour into the base glaze.

Overglaze Colours

Sometimes known as 'on-glaze' colours, these are enamels that are painted over the fired glaze, which is then refired to between 690°C and 750°C. Really bright reds and yellows can be obtained using these enamels, but the methods of application are very sophisticated and unless one has a great deal of skill and patience the results can look very crude. This method of decoration is not used in our studio; very few people like to use these colours, and we have no room to store the decorated pots while we wait for enough to fill the kiln for the third firing.

116. Mary Adkins, white earthenware birds. Underglaze paints mixed with glaze and painted over white opaque base glaze

Glossary

Banding wheel—a small hand-operated wheel used to facilitate building by hand and for use in decoration. Sometimes called a whirler.

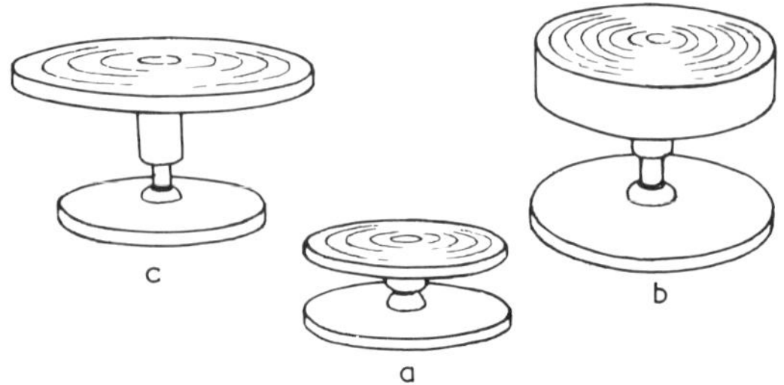

117. Banding wheels as supplied by Fulham Pottery: *a* light aluminium whirler; *b* heavy aluminium whirler; *c* cast-iron whirler

Bat, batt—a porous board on which to work clay. Often shaped to fit a wheel-head.
—kiln shelf.
Bat wash—protective covering for kiln shelves.
Biscuit, bisque—term used to refer to unglazed, once-fired clay.
Blistering—formation of bubbles in a glaze, often caused by an excess of a metallic oxide.
Body—any clay or mixture of clay and filler that can be used to make pottery.
Burnishing—polishing the surface of leather-hard clay.
Bush fire—an open bonfire in which pots are fired.
Calabash—a kind of gourd that has a very hard skin. Used to hold water and for dry storage.
Carbonisation—impregnation of a pot with carbon. Occurs only under reducing conditions, such as those produced in a sawdust firing.
Caustic substance—a substance that has a corroding and disintegrating effect on the skin.
Cheese wire—a length of wire or nylon gut with a handle at each end, used for cutting clay.
Colloidal—so finely divided as to remain in suspension when mixed with water.
Cratering—the formation of small craters on the surface of fired ware. These are caused by nodules within the clay which, when heated, expand to a much greater extent than the body itself.

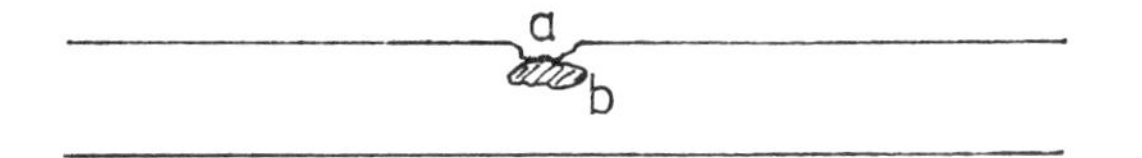

118. Cratering: *a* crater; *b* nodule causing the crater

Crawling—a glaze defect in which the glaze tends to contract into separate masses instead of spreading evenly. Can be caused by dust or grease on the surface before glazing, or by too thick an application of glaze. Sometimes produced deliberately as a decorative feature on double-dipped ware.

Crazing—the formation of a network of fine cracks in a glaze, caused by the glaze contracting to a greater extent than the body of the pot.

Distortion—the warping of clay during drying or firing, caused by stresses set up in the clay owing to uneven thickness, texture or drying.

Dunting—cracking caused by too rapid heating or cooling of biscuit ware.

Earthenware—fired clay that remains porous.

Filler—any inert material, such as silica sand or grog, that can be added to a body to increase its strength and resistance to thermal shock and to reduce warping and shrinkage.

Firing temperature—the temperature at which a glaze or body reaches maturity.

Fit—equality of expansion and contraction between a glaze and a body, which are said to fit each other.

Flashing—accidental partial reduction or carbonisation of part of a pot.

Flux—a substance that lowers the melting point of a substance. A glaze is said to flux well when it melts to form a very mobile liquid.

Fly ash—ash carried through a kiln by draughts from the firebox.

Fritt—a selection of minerals fired to fuse them together and then ground to form a powder which is used as the basis of a glaze. This is the method by which water-soluble fluxes are made available for use in glazes. The process is also used to lessen the toxicity of certain minerals, such as lead, by combining them with silica.

Glaze—a powder covering, applied to biscuit ware, which when fired produces a glassy covering on the ware.

Glaze mop—a large, very soft brush, used to apply glaze to ware.

Glost firing—the firing of glazed ware.

Green ware—unfired pottery.

Grog—ground biscuit-fired clay used as a filler or for texturing.

Kiln—an enclosed oven of any kind that will fire clay to above 600°C.

Lawn brush—a robust brush used to push glaze or slip through a sieve.

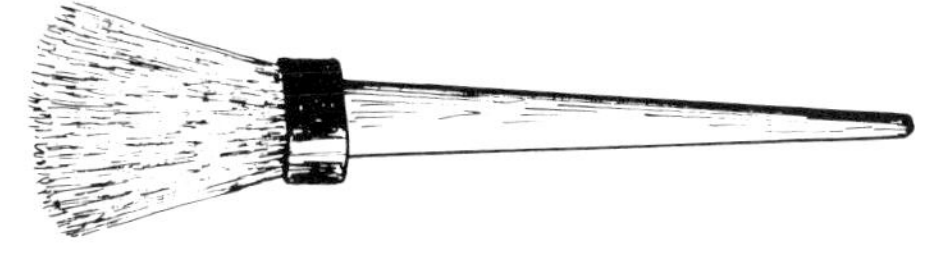

119. Lawn brush

Lawn sieve—a sieve in which the mesh is made from phosphor bronze.

Leather-hard—the term used for clay which is too dry to bend without cracking but is still soft enough for shavings to be pared from its surface using a knife.

Majolica—a method of decorating pottery by painting metallic oxides on to a tin white glaze.

Maturing temperature—the temperature at which a glaze becomes sufficiently fluid to form a smooth even layer over the body that it is to cover.

Opalescence—a cloudy, semi-transparent effect in glaze.

Opaque glaze—a glaze that completely conceals the colour of the body that it covers.

Oxidising atmosphere—the atmosphere inside a kiln when oxygen is present during firing.

Palette knife—a very thin-bladed flexible knife without a specific cutting edge.

Pitting—*see* cratering.

Prop—a purpose-made pillar used to support shelves within a kiln.

Pugged—de-aired and consolidated.

Pugmill—machine for producing pugged clay.

Raku—a Japanese ceremony in which glazed pots are taken from the kiln while the glaze is still molten, and covered with sawdust to achieve reduction of the glaze or plunged straight into water to produce rapid cooling effects.

Reconstitution—the process by which used unfired clay is reconditioned for use.

Reducing atmosphere—the atmosphere inside a kiln when all available oxygen has been removed by combustion.

Reduction—the process by which oxides are reduced by the removal of oxygen atoms. For example, copper oxide can be reduced to the pure metal, while iron oxides are reduced from those containing two or three atoms of oxygen per molecule to those containing only one.

Refractory substances—those which will withstand very high temperatures and corrosion.

Shivering—the flaking of glaze which occurs when the body contracts more than the glaze which covers it.

Short-textured—the term used for clay which is not very plastic and tends to crumble when worked. Plastic clays can show this quality if they are overworked or their moisture content is too low.

Silica sand—a very fine pure sand used in pottery as a protective covering for kiln shelves and as a filler.

Slip—liquid clay used as a cement to join leather-hard clay, and as decoration.

Slip-casting—a means of mass production by which articles are made by pouring slip into plaster moulds.

Stoneware—a clay that withstands being fired to between 1200°C and 1350°C without collapsing. At this temperature it becomes impermeable and partly vitrified. Stoneware clay generally has a very low iron content, as iron tends to act as a flux, causing vitrification and distortion.

Tan liquor—a solution made by boiling oak bark or tea in water, used to provide a finish on pots fired in a bush fire.

Terracotta—unglazed red earthenware.

Thermal shock—the sudden application of heat, causing uneven expansion in an object that can lead to its breakage.

Throwing—making pots on a revolving wheel-head.

Tooling—the trimming of leather-hard clay; usually applied to the neatening of the foot or rim of a wheel-thrown pot.

Toxic—poisonous.

Transparent glaze—a glaze through which the clay body can be seen.

Unstable glaze—a glaze that is not prepared to a balanced formula and is therefore liable to change chemically and physically after being fired, especially when in contact with acid or alkaline solutions.

Vitrification—the complete fusion of a substance to form a glass. Total vitrification of a body generally leads to its collapse, except in the case of porcelain. Although it is an improper use of the word, a stoneware clay that has been fired until it is impermeable is said to be vitrified.

Warping—*see* distortion.

Wedging—the method by which clay is worked by hand to remove air pockets and to promote an even texture throughout.

Wheel, potter's wheel—a foot- or power-driven wheel on which to throw pots.

Whirler—*see* banding wheel.

Appendix 1: Safety Precautions

Many raw materials used in pottery-making are injurious to health. Finely divided silica, present in most prepared clay bodies and glazes, can cause silicosis if inhaled. Colouring oxides, with the exception of the iron oxides, should all be treated as poisonous, and all of them are dangerous if the powder is inhaled.

The risks involved can be minimised if the following rules are adhered to.

1. Do not smoke or eat in the workshop.
2. Use a covered sieve when sifting dry raw materials or, if this is not possible, wear a mask and work outside. If this sort of work is done out in the open, a dusty atmosphere within the pottery can be avoided.
3. Break up dry clay in the open or, if this is not possible, between two sheets of strong polythene.
4. Keep the floor clean using a vacuum cleaner with a disposable filter bag rather than trying to sweep with a brush.
5. Use a damp rag or plastic foam for cleaning tables and shelving. Single wipes with a damp sponge, rinsing it between each wipe, are more effective than a scrubbing motion using a lot of water.
6. Clean all equipment using a damp sponge or rag.
7. Do not spray slips, glazes or suspended oxides in the workshop unless a special cabinet with an extractor fan is used.
8. Scrub hands and fingernails after work, especially when colouring materials and glazes have been in use.
9. Transfer all dry materials and glazes to rigid labelled containers with lids. If left in sacks or paper bags they often become contaminated, and the bags get dusty and damaged. When a sack or bag is opened, the contents are disturbed and create dust. Storage in rigid containers helps to lessen the dust problem.

Above all, common sense and cleanliness are the two most important factors in the running of a safe pottery.

Appendix 2: Exhibitions

About every eighteen months the Camperdown students hold a two-day exhibition of their work. This teaches them how to organise and stage such events and enables them to sell things they might wish to part with. It also gives them confidence in their work if pieces are sold. We make a note of any outstanding work produced during the interval between exhibitions, and in due course these articles are returned for exhibition, together with any pieces that the potters wish to sell. The first day is an evening affair with a buffet supper and preview by invitation, with someone of importance to open the exhibition. During the evening an auction is held to sell some of the best pieces. The second day is open to the public.

The funds raised at the last two exhibitions have gone towards the building of the potters' own ceramics workshop (see Appendix 3).

Four weeks before the date set for the exhibition, each student is given two questionnaires, one concerning the staging and management of the exhibition, and the other concerning the provision of food and the running of the buffet supper. The replies to these questions are tabulated, and adjustments are made if necessary to cover under- or over-manning and to prevent too much of a particular food being provided. (If there is a surfeit of food it is sold off at the end of the auction.) Once this initial organisation has been done, each student is left to carry out the tasks of his choice. A person is chosen to take responsibility for each section, including the staging, the raffle and the auction, and with everyone knowing what to do and when to do it we have held some very successful and enjoyable events.

QUESTIONNAIRE: Exhibition

1. Name
2. Can you help stage on Thursday 10am—1pm
   2pm—4pm
   4pm—6pm
3. Can you deliver your pottery to the centre on Wednesday between 7pm and 9pm?
4. Have you any pieces you wish to sell?
5. Will you price them?
6. What % do you wish to go to the funds? (minimum 25%)
7. Can you steward or sell raffle tickets on Saturday?
   10am—12noon
   12noon—2pm
   2pm—4pm

8. Can you collect your pottery and help to clear up 4pm on Saturday?
9. If not, can you arrange for someone else to do so?
10. Can you draw some posters to put up around the town?

QUESTIONNAIRE: Exhibition Buffet Supper

A. Can you come?
B. Would you like to:
   a. sell raffle tickets
   b. mingle and talk to guests
   c. help with auction
   d. man the entrance to collect tickets and money for those unpaid.
C. Camperdown students will be admitted free on condition that they provide some food towards the buffet supper. Please tick items you can provide and state quantity.
   1. Cheese
   2. Bread rolls, white
      brown
      French bread
   3. Butter
   4. Small sausage rolls
   5. Cocktail sausages on sticks
   6. Cheese biscuits
   7. Paté
   8. Washed celery
   9. Watercress
   10. Fruit of any kind
   11. Pickled gherkins
   12. Pickled onions
   13. Olives
   14. Cheese dips
   15. Tablecloths (large coloured sheets)
   16. Flower arrangements for tables
   17. Any other suggestions
D. Can you help with preparation of food and tables 5pm—7pm Friday evening?
E. When can you deliver the food to the centre?
F. Can you bring it prepared on a plate etc?
G. Will you collect the plate at the end of the evening?
H. How many tickets do you need for sale to friends (or relatives)?

Appendix 3: The Ceramics Workshop

Because of a lack of finance or suitable accommodation, it is not always possible for fully trained students to set up on their own. In this case, it is a good idea for a group to form a club and to build a communal workshop, as some of our former students have done.

At the end of 1976, our third-year students were fortunate enough to obtain permission from the Devon County Council Education Committee to convert the disused rifle range at the Leisure Centre (formerly the Drill Hall) in Exmouth into a pottery. This was to be somewhere for students to continue work after they left the Camperdown Pottery. They were granted permission on a 'do-it-yourself' basis, with no financial help from the County, and on certain conditions. First, the workshop had to be made available for the use of residents from Davey Court, a rest home for blind and disabled persons. This was because the home was to supply a kiln which had been purchased by a group of blind people, taught to make pottery by the present authors, who had been moved to Davey Court when their former home and pottery were closed. Secondly, students from other Adult Education classes in the area were to be allowed to join the club if they possessed the necessary qualifications.

The potters formed themselves into a club with the necessary constitution and, either individually or in groups, set out to raise an estimated £1,200 needed for building and equipping the workshop. They did this by means of jumble sales, coffee mornings, sales of work and raffles.

Under the guidance of the chairman, Brian Adams, work was started on the dismantling of the rifle range, and as soon as money was available, the building and fitting of the workshop began. This was done on a rota basis, and wives, husbands and friends with special skills were called upon to help as well. Only six months after the initial permission had been granted, the workshop was complete. It is now in constant use, with all working amicably together and no one specifically in charge. A group of residents from Davey Court attend a pottery session once a week, supervised by former Camperdown potters.

The first annual general meeting was held in May 1978, and the club is now well established and a very good example of self-sufficiency.

The following is the 'Potters' Charter', which is displayed prominently in the workshop.

Leisure Centre Ceramic Workshop

This workshop is used by members and their guests in a spirit of goodwill towards each other. We all do our best to co-operate with each other by leaving everything in its proper place and in a state of cleanliness, neatness and with due regard for the nature of the material and equipment we use. However, no one of us knows everything; we can all learn from each other by watching, listening and asking. Nobody is in charge. We all make mistakes and we are all learning. If you make a mistake which may affect somebody else, please tell someone or ask for advice before the mistake leads to another person's work being spoilt. Nobody will be criticised.

Brian Adams
Chairman

Appendix 4: Suppliers of Pottery Materials

Great Britain

General Suppliers

Ferro (Great Britain) Ltd, Wombourne, Wolverhampton
The Fulham Pottery Ltd, 110 New Kings Road, London SW6 4NY
Harrison Mayer Ltd, 105 Minet Road, London SW9 7UH
Podmore Ceramics Ltd, 105 Minet Road, London SW9 7UH
Podmore & Sons Ltd, Shelton, Stoke-on-Trent ST1 4PQ
Wengers Ltd, Etruria, Stoke-on-Trent ST4 7BQ

Gas Burner Equipment

Wm A. Meyer Ltd, 9/11 Gleneldon Road, Streatham, London SW16 2AU

Kilns

Cromartie Kilns Ltd, Park Hall Road, Longton, Stoke-on-Trent ST3 5AY

Clay and Kiln Furniture

Acme Marls Ltd, Clough Street, Hanley, Stoke-on-Trent

Overseas Suppliers

Most of the following firms supply grogged buff, red and raku bodies which should be suitable for bush firing and for firing in the updraft and makeshift gas kilns.

Australia

Ferro Corporation (Aust) Pty Ltd, 16 Bermill Street, Rockdale, New South Wales

Harrison Mayer Craft & Education, 33 Adrian Street, Welshpool, Western Australia 6106

AGENTS FOR FULHAM POTTERY

Nonporite (WA) Pty Ltd, PO Box 19, Hamilton Hill, Western Australia 6163

Walker Ceramics, Boronia Road, Wantirnam, Victoria 3152

R. G. Williams & Co Pty Ltd, 50/52 Geddes Street, Mulgrave, Victoria 3170

AGENTS FOR PODMORE & SONS LTD

Russell Cowan Pty Ltd, 128/138 Pacific Highway, Waitara, New South Wales 2077

AGENTS FOR WENGERS LTD

Mrs S. McNeil, Diamond Ceramic Supplies, 12 Bridge Street, Rydalmere, New South Wales 2116

The Potters Workshop, 28 Greenaway, Bulleen 3105, Victoria

Pottery Supplies, 262 Given Terrace, Paddington, Brisbane 4064, Queensland

Ceramic Art Supplies, Thorngate Basement Building (SE), 57 Pulteney Street, Adelaide 5000

New Zealand

Ferro Plastics (NZ) Ltd, PO Box 30066, Poland Road, Takapuna, Auckland

AGENT FOR HARRISON MAYER LTD

Screen Printing & Ceramic Supplies Ltd, PO Box 30-180, Lower Hutt

AGENTS FOR PODMORE & SONS LTD

D. Hourigan Ltd (CCG Industries Ltd), 33 Crowhurst Street, PO Box 3724, Newmarket, Auckland 1

Southern Ceramic Import Co, Main Road, Lorneville, No 6 RD Invercargill

AGENTS FOR WENGERS LTD

Smith & Smith Ltd, PO Box 709, Auckland North

Smith & Smith Ltd, PO Box 2196, Wellington (North)

Smith & Smith Ltd, PO Box 22496, High Street, Christchurch

United States of America

American Art Clay Co Inc, 4717 West 16th Street, Indianapolis, Indiana 46222

Ferro Corporation, International Division, Erieview Plaza, Cleveland, Ohio 44114

Index